ARE YOU DUMB ENOUGH TO BE RICH?

THE AMAZINGLY SIMPLE WAY TO MAKE MILLIONS IN REAL ESTATE

G. WILLIAM BARNETT II

FOREWORD BY
ROBERT G. ALLEN

AMACOM **AMERICAN MANAGEMENT ASSOCIATION**
NEW YORK ♦ ATLANTA ♦ BRUSSELS ♦ BUENOS AIRES
CHICAGO ♦ LONDON ♦ MEXICO CITY ♦ SAN FRANCISCO
SHANGHAI ♦ TOKYO ♦ TORONTO ♦ WASHINGTON, D.C.

Special discounts on bulk quantities of AMACOM books are available to corporations, professional associations, and other organizations. For details, contact Special Sales Department, AMACOM, a division of American Management Association, 1601 Broadway, New York, NY 10019.
Tel.: 212-903-8316. Fax: 212-903-8083.
Web site: www.amacombooks.org

This publication is designed to provide accurate and authoritative information in regard to the subject matter covered. It is sold with the understanding that the publisher is not engaged in rendering legal, accounting, or other professional service. If legal advice or other expert assistance is required, the services of a competent professional person should be sought.

Library of Congress Cataloging-in-Publication Data

Barnett, G. William.
  Are you dumb enough to be rich? : the amazingly simple way to make millions in real estate / G. William Barnett II.
    p. cm.
Includes index.
ISBN 0-8144-7177-3
1. Real estate investment—United States. I. Title.

HD255.B376 2003
332.63'24'0973—dc21

2003000646

Printing number

10 9 8 7 6 5 4 3 2 1

CONTENTS

This book is dedicated to the one through whom all things are possible, my Lord and Savior Jesus Christ. Thank you for my countless blessings.

ACKNOWLEDGEMENTS

The writing, compiling and editing of *Are You Dumb Enough to Be Rich?* has taken over three years. As with any project of this magnitude there have been many self discoveries and opportunities for growth. Throughout my life and this process there have been important contributors. I want to thank the following people:

My family. To Kris, I love you with all my heart and deeply appreciate you putting up with all the late nights, early mornings and time on the road.

To Trey, my oldest son, you are my inspiration. Your dedication to being the best you can be continually sets a great example for me. I love you and I am so proud of you. I only wish that every father could experience a son like you.

To my baby boy, Bryce, you are my motivation. Everyday is such a treat to see those sparkling eyes and that smile, your unconditional love puts everything else in perspective. Daddy loves you.

To my Mother and Father, Muriel and George Barnett for the example of what great parents are. Your continued support and encouragement is a guiding light for our entire family.

To both of my brothers, Johnny and Tommy, for taking care of little brother, no matter what my age is.

To my Aunt Joyce Lowther for always being in my corner.

To my late grandmother and uncle. "Nannie," you always told me how special I was, and coming from you, I believed it. To my Uncle "T," so much of my personal and professional style came from you. I always wanted to grow up and be like my Uncle "T."

To Mark Victor Hansen for believing in me and pushing me to get the "DUMB Enough" message out. For more than twenty years you have been there as a role model and mentor.

To Robert Allen for taking me by the hand and showing me how to write a book from beginning to end. Thanks also for kicking my speaking career into high gear.

To Ron LeGrand for your teaching, friendship and allowing me the opportunity to share my personal beliefs through the "One Hour Destiny" from your platform.

To Dave Yoho for believing in me before I believed in myself.

To Ray O'Connell at Amacom, for your guidance in the writing and editing process. You added a lot without being overbearing. This is a better book thanks to you.

Over the years there have been many great mentors and friends. I'd like to publicly thank you: Jim and Melba Rupe, Roger Kerbow, Gene and Lana Turner, Ty and Pat Boyd, Thomas Ed Lawhon, Brad Barker, Travis Tindal, Jon and Amy Kubas, Mark Dove, David Cooper and Bill Cantrell. Your friendship and encouragement is the mark of a true friend and I am blessed to have each of you.

FOREWORD

As you peruse this book you may be thinking, "Who needs another book about real estate investing?" I must admit I thought, "Is this just another 'me-too' book in an already overcrowded field?"

No! Bill Barnett's unique voice makes a compelling read. Anyone interested in accumulating wealth through real estate will benefit from his 120-day, foolproof, step-by-step method.

I'm proud to call Bill both a student and a friend. In *Are You Dumb Enough to Be Rich?* he encapsulates my life's work: teaching others the principles of achieving wealth and financial freedom.

Chances are that, like me, you are part of the baby boomer generation. We are part of the first group of Americans for whom putting our kids through college has spiraled out of control, often beyond $100,000 for a four-year degree. Social Security can no longer be depended upon as in past generations. Credit card debt has millions of Americans in a financial vise.

These facts make it imperative that we learn the skills that will allow us to break free of the bondage of debt and financial lack. For the average man or woman, financial freedom can be achieved faster through real estate than any other investment.

In my five best sellers, *Nothing Down, Creating Wealth, Multiple Streams of Income, Multiple Streams of Internet Income,* and my latest, co-authored with Mark Victor Hansen, *One Minute Millionaire,* the objective is to guide you down the path to financial freedom. One of those paths is real estate. And Bill Barnett's 120-Day Plan provides an excellent road map. What Bill teaches is not theory. It is fact. I know it works because real estate is how I made my first million.

Enjoy this journey of discovery and learn whether you truly are

DUMB Enough to Be RICH.

Robert G. Allen

PREFACE

You've made the wonderful decision to start your real estate investing career. Maybe you've noticed the housing market boom in the last few years. Maybe you're just smart and realize how lucrative real estate investing can be. Or maybe you lost money in the stock market (like most of us) and you just want a more secure investment—one that's backed by actual property.

In any event, you've picked up this book to find out how you can become rich from real estate. Congratulations—you've already taken an intelligent step toward starting out right in real estate. You've decided to use this book as a guide to some of the real estate secrets and to find out how to avoid the most common pitfalls.

Organization of the Book

In each of the chapters that follow there will be a "Pitfalls" segment to let you know some of the pitfalls to avoid in your real estate investing career. As your mentor, I will personally guide you around some of these pitfalls, saving you money, time, and heartache. This is one of the primary benefits of this book. Be careful how you choose your mentors because their advice can mean extra hundreds of thousands, even millions, of dollars to you.

This book is laid out as an action plan for the beginning investor and the investor who may have some experience but not enough success to make a life-changing difference. I call it an autobiographical textbook. I will personally guide you through daily activities and action steps for the first 120 days of your new investing career. One hundred and twenty days should be enough time to get you through that all-important first deal.

Why Real Estate?

No other investment strategy has created more millionaires than investing in real estate. I used the investment strategy outlined in this book and became an asset millionaire in 120 days. This book will help you make those first tentative steps into a secure and bountiful financial future in 120 days.

INTRODUCTION

BANG! An explosion went off in my head as real as if a shotgun had gone off next to my ear. I sat straight up in my bed. Having clarity at 5 A.M. is not easy, but this was different. I was awakened from a deep and restful sleep. The sound in my head had not startled me. It had *started* me. I realized at that moment, "I get it! I understand! I am DUMB Enough to Be RICH!" As I sat on my bed, a feeling of pure adrenaline rushed through me, and at the same time there was a sense of calm. I knew at that moment everything was going to be OK.

Frustration and anxiety had built up for the past twelve years. Having worked as a stockbroker at a leading firm and then moved into the financial services arena of a major savings and loan, I was considered by most to be successful. I was in that elusive one percent of wage earners, the ones that make a six-figure-plus income so routinely it becomes boring.

Then an opportunity appeared. One of my closest friends and another associate decided to open a "boutique" investment banking firm in Texas. I seized the opportunity. I was moving back to God's country. My entrepreneurial juices were flowing again. Within days I had packed my belongings and was on an airplane, heading into a new area of expertise and with one of my closest friends to boot. Our new three-way partnership rocked along just fine for three years. In fact, we even brought in a fourth partner to help handle the growing business. I oversaw the build-out of our 5,200-square-foot luxury offices in the brand-new ballpark in Arlington, Texas. The ballpark is home to major league baseball's Texas Rangers, and I could sit at my new cherry wood executive desk and look out over center field. We had a balcony where I could walk right out to watch the games without even buying a ticket. Life was good.

It was during this time that we evaluated a company for investment purposes. The company was located in northern California and bought inner-city houses to refurbish. After the houses were put in top condition, the company would sell them while carrying the mortgage. This created a tidy profit and the constant need for more cash. We passed on making an investment in this company because the partners thought it was too boring. I, however, was hooked. I thought about this company many times over the next few months.

Mid-summer arrived in Texas. That meant dog days, a wonderful six-week stretch where the temperature rarely went below 100 degrees. The custom around our office was for all of us to go to lunch together. Our excuse was that lunch provided us with a time to get business done without phone interruptions. I don't know if anyone bought this bull, but we needed to justify it to ourselves. On this particular Friday, a Friday that didn't seem any different from all the others, it was closing in on 11:30 A.M.—lunchtime. We had all started gathering our things to head out when one of the partners said we needed to step into the conference room for a quick meeting. It was there that I walked into a nasty little round of mutiny and betrayal.

My three partners, led by the guy who was as close to me as a brother, decided they didn't want me as a partner any longer. They actually used the words "You're fired. " I said, "You can't fire me, you don't pay me."

There it was: My good friend had worked most of the night before putting this scheme together and convincing the other two I should be ousted. As I write this five years later, I still do not know what happened. But success is the best revenge, so to my former partners I must say "Thank you." Without their actions I would have stayed involved and I would not be where I am today. God does indeed work in mysterious ways.

Over the next few weeks I pondered what I should do. Thinking about that real estate company my partners had passed on was one thing; acting on it was altogether something else. I phoned my contact for the company and said I was interested in developing the same type of company in the Dallas-Fort Worth area. My contact thought it was a good idea and said he would talk to a member of senior management at the company. When he called, he shared with me that the senior manager he was trying to contact had left the company and might be looking for a new opportunity. After a couple of three-way conference calls, we decided to join forces and start the company.

Now we had a company consisting of two guys who had no experience and a former member of senior management at a company doing millions of dollars worth of business. Of the three of us, I was broke. One of the others had about $40,000 worth of cash and credit, and our ex-senior manager had no money and no credit.

PITFALL: GOING PARTNER CRAZY

So here's your first pitfall: Many of us who start a new venture believe that we need partners. It must have something to do with not wanting to be alone or creating a team. Maybe it's that we have been taught that two heads are better than one. Napoleon Hill, in his classic *Think and Grow Rich,* states, "No two minds ever come together without, thereby, creating a third invisible, intangible force which may be likened to a third mind." And while I agree totally with the teachings of Mr. Hill, we must be careful whom we select as partners.

Make sure that if you are hell-bent on having partners, your partners bring something meaningful—either skill or cash—to the table. Two or three broke, inexperienced people getting together to start a company simply means the company is broke and none of the partners have mastered the ability to make money. Two or three weak links do not make for a strong chain. In my case, three guys with $40,000 between them and what I later discovered was almost meaningless experience from our self-appointed guru, the senior manager, does not make for a strong partnership.

In hindsight, my lack of education in the real estate investing arena cost me three years of frustration and probably well over $100,000. This could easily have been avoided by simply going to the bookstore and buying a hundred dollars or so of knowledge that is readily available. I commend you on doing this and assure you that this book will save you money, time, and heartache.

The challenge was before us: We had to raise more money. After all, we had three mouths to feed and everyone knows that you can't start a business without a bunch of cash. Since I came from an investment banking background, this part was pretty simple to me.

We wrote a business plan and called some of my money contacts, one of whom brought in a client of his for $75,000 cash. Of course both he and his client wanted a piece of the company. And they got it. Our little start-up had grown from just me to two, then three and now five partners and we had just purchased our first piece of property. The five were made up of three people who were supposed to work and two silent partners. You have probably already figured out that my piece of the company had shrunk dramatically. There is an old investment-banking adage that says, "A small piece of a big pie is worth more than all of a small pie." Somehow I had managed to negotiate an ever-shrinking piece of a small pie.

As one of my mentors, the late, truly great Cavett Robert, once said, "Bill, this is an idea that is born dead." What he meant was that our company was underfunded, top-heavy, and had so many mouths to feed that there was little chance of its surviving. Just prior to bringing in the half-million-dollar credit line, we enjoyed the excitement of having our first bid on a property being accepted. It took four months of hard work for us to find that first deal.

Of course in those few short months we were out of money, so the logical thing to do was to raise more money. This time I brought in *another* partner who gave the company a $500,000 credit line. Does this sound like the old business joke about making it up in volume?

Just prior to bringing in the half million dollars, we had been able to purchase a Housing and Urban Development (HUD) home and rehabilitate it. With all the mistakes we made and all the overpriced contractors we used, we still made a $20,000 profit on the sale. Upon finding our buyer and working them patiently through the mortgage maze, I thought everything was going to be great.

We had just closed on the property earlier that morning and I had a cashier's check from the title company. We were on our way.

Then the phone rang. It was the homeowner and he explained that he, his wife, and the moving company were in front of the house and could not get in. This was on a Monday and it was now midday. I assured the new buyers that I had gone by on Friday and checked all the locks and keys and they worked fine. "No Bill, you don't understand," said the frustrated buyer, "we cannot get in because one of your partners has been on a drinking binge and has barricaded himself in the house."

Excuse me. Have we entered "The Twilight Zone"? Could you repeat that please?

Unfortunately, we had to call the police to resolve the problem. It was my intention from the day the company was formed to become a famous real estate investor. This just wasn't the way I had planned it. So there I was: My first deal had just closed and I was already on the evening news. To say the least, it was an unusual beginning to my new real estate entrepreneurial adventure. Over the next few days, this partner was removed from the equation and life went on.

In the meantime, my other partner had taken a job and was now working full time. Let's check our scorecard—Bill does all the work and gets to enjoy splitting the profits with three silent partners now.

All of that for $75,000 of borrowed money and an outrageously expensive credit line. *What was I thinking?* With this credit line, another silent partner was removed from the mix. Now the working formula hadn't changed. There I was doing all the work and splitting the profits with three silent partners.

All of that partner mess could have been avoided. You do not need partners, a large credit line, or a bunch of cash to become a highly successful real estate investor. One of the first tests you'll have to pass to discover if you are truly Dumb Enough to Be Rich is whether or not you can accept the truth in the previous statement. If you can't, put the book down and go on about your life just the way it is. But if you can, take a deep breath and move forward knowing that becoming wealthy as a real estate investor can be achieved without the traditional trappings of a start-up company.

If you overthink the whole process, you won't get there. Congrats, for all of you still reading this information. It could save you three years of investing in real estate the wrong way—the old-fashioned way. Just keep saying to yourself, "Dumb for 120 puts me on the road to plenty!"

For the next twenty-eight months I worked exclusively in the Housing and Urban Development market. How to work in this segment of the industry is covered in detail in Chapter 6.

I was growing restless. This was not how I had pictured my life and my company developing. The money was finally good, but all I had succeeded in doing was trading one trap for another. I was not on the road to true financial freedom. I had not yet become Dumb Enough to Be Rich.

During this time, I had started dating a wonderful woman. We fell deeply in love, and she had accepted my proposal of marriage. We were closing in on our April 1st wedding date. I know, you're probably thinking what is anyone doing getting married on April Fool's Day? Due to her work schedule, the only options for April were for the 1st or the 15th. Now don't get me wrong—I love our country deeply, but there wasn't anything romantic I could think of about celebrating our wedding anniversary on April 15th, Tax Day. So, April 15th went out the window and April 1st it was.

We're not talking ancient history here; this was April of 2000. That's an important fact to remember. You need to know that the principles of buying and selling real estate creatively work today, right now, right where you are.

As our wedding approached, I began to feel a tremendous sense of anxiety. The business wasn't growing the way I wanted it to, and it was consuming me. If our lives stayed the same as we went forward, we would have a good life. That's not what I wanted; I wanted my wife and family to have a *great* life, not just a good life.

I started looking for better ways to be a real estate investor, ways to make more money with less hassle, to build a business that did not require my full attention twenty-four hours a day, seven days a week. In my quest for information, I started ordering courses from television. It sounded good and it wasn't too expensive. After several courses and several thousand dollars worth of materials, nothing changed.

In the meantime, I started attending the Dallas AIREO (Association of Independent Real Estate Owners). AIREO is a group of local real estate investors that meets monthly and has a program on real estate investing. This is an excellent way to meet other real estate investors and create a good referral network. If you are not aware of an investment club in your area, start asking around or search the Internet. Finding an investment club in your area will be a great resource to you. If there isn't one in your area, start one. Visit the Dallas AIREO's Web site at www.AIREO.com and e-mail your questions on starting your own club. As Mark Victor Hansen says, "As your network grows, your net worth grows." An investment club will help you locate resources such as a tenant checking company.

As your business grows and you recognize the need to acquire some rental property, for the tax advantages if nothing else, you will need a tenant checking company to research potential tenants. Such companies screen your tenants for you. But investment clubs can offer other benefits as well.

I learned one of the most important lessons of selling homes in just such an investment club. (The speaker that evening was Robyn Thompson, known as "the Queen of Rehabs.") At the time, I had two houses I couldn't sell. I discovered that I was marketing them wrong. Though my fliers used beautiful fonts and flashy photographs of the property, I wasn't getting any calls. Robyn showed me that to attract buyers I had to appeal to their wallets. Facts and figures about the mortgage attract more interested buyers than lengthy descriptions of the house or photographs. I reconstructed my fliers to look like Figure 1-1 to test out this new method.

Surprisingly, the number of calls concerning the properties went up dramatically. Within thirty-one days of changing my fliers, both houses were sold. I do not mean they were under contract. I mean they were sold, the sales had closed, and the money was in my pocket.

The closings were two days apart. It was 5:00 A.M. on the morning after the first closing when the Bang! happened and I knew I was going to be rich.

The clarity of that thought was invigorating. I understood at the core of my being what my mentors had been saying all along. I will no longer be too smart for my own good. I will continue to seek out new information and people to learn from them and accept their teachings. I will not simply dismiss what they are saying because I haven't done it their way. I will have the courage to try it myself. I will be Dumb Enough to Be Rich.

Your company name and address
Phone number

Home for Sale!
Address of home

Price

Very brief description of the property

IT CAN BE YOURS FOR ONLY $XXX.00 PER MONTH!

First-Time Buyers May Only Need   **$XXX.00**

Mortgage   **$XXX.00**
Tax   **$XXX.00**
Insurance   **$XX.00**
Mortgage Insurance   **$XX.00**

NO DOWN PAYMENT!
NO CLOSING COSTS!

More than 5,000 people will get this notice! Don't miss out! Call now! The numbers above are for illustrative purposes only. Rates, points, and fees cannot be guaranteed. All numbers are based on approved credit.

FIGURE 1-1

Chapter Summary

If you want to be a millionaire, you have got to listen to millionaires and not your next-door neighbor or that goofball at work. That is what I am asking you to do with this material, accept it as not only possible, but achievable. Make the leap. It works—use it to change your life for the better.

In the next chapter, you'll be introduced to the mindset of a millionaire and learn how to prevent anyone from stealing your tent.

Pitfalls Recap

GOING PARTNER CRAZY. Be careful whom you select as partners. Make sure that if you are hell-bent on having partners, your partners bring something meaningful—either skill or cash—to the table.

THE MINDSET
OF A MILLIONAIRE...
OR SOMEONE STOLE OUR TENT

THE FIRST THING you must do on your quest to financial freedom is to decide what you want your business to provide and what you are willing to do to accomplish that.

This type of thinking is "The Millionaire's Mindset," because you won't find a millionaire who made his or her money alone who didn't have a strong sense of financial direction. Remember, know the objective and the path will reveal itself. For the sake of this book, I am going to assume that you want to become a millionaire and you want to do it through real estate investments. In their best-seller, *The Millionaire Next Door*, Ph.D.'s Thomas Stanley and William Danko make an interesting prediction concerning the number of millionaire households in the United States. It is their contention that by the year 2005, the number of millionaire households will grow to a whopping 5,625,408. The exciting part of this prediction is the word "households." There are slightly more than 100 million households in the United States. That means that more than 5 percent of the households will reach millionaire status in the next few years. It also means that a lot of people have achieved this, and you can too. Five point six million households is a lot of households. Make the decision now that you are going to be one of those millionaire households. You must first make the commitment before you can start making the money.

There is no other investment that comes close to producing the sheer number of millionaires as real estate. There is no other investment that can introduce you to millionaire rates of return easier than real estate. It is the safest and fastest way to millionaire status I know of *if you do it the right way*. Doing it the right way is what this book is all about.

So, how do we become one of the millionaire households? How do we attain the Millionaire's Mindset? In my success training course, "The One Hour Destiny," I show attendees how to brainstorm their success for twenty minutes a day. All of these success tips amount to one thing—you have to write it down.

Of all of the aforementioned success giants, the one that hammered this message home for me is someone you most likely have never heard of. Her instruction to me was to write "I will not talk in class" 101 times on the board after school. You see, repetition is *the* secret to success. The words kept ringing in my head as I wrote it on the board in Ms. Simpson's eighth-grade English class at West Point Junior High School in West Point, Mississippi. This was my punishment for not being attentive in class and distracting others from doing their work. Of course, I probably spent as much time counting the number of sentences I had written as I did writing. This seemed like a never-ending task, but I became resolved never to do this again, which means, *I will not talk in class* in the future either.

This principle, *I will not talk in class,* is a major key to success. It distills the essence of several key ingredients to successful goal setting and goal achieving.

First, it is a written affirmation. Certainly in the quest for success, your studies have revealed that you must write down your goals. The simple act of writing cements the goals in your subconscious. All of the great trainers and speakers preach that you have to write it down.

PITFALL: I DON'T HAVE TO WRITE THEM DOWN

It is right here that most people fail to move forward. You're probably thinking, "I don't really have to write them down, I know what they are. I think about them all the time." It is these little things that make the difference between success and failure, moderate success or roaring success. Commit—*right now*—to me and to yourself: I will do whatever it takes to reach my goals. I will not stop even if it means I have to write them down.

For me it was Ms. Simpson who drove home this vital point with her instruction to write I will not talk in class 101 times on the board. The thought began to permeate my being. Not only did I not want to be punished this way again, but for the rest of the school year and throughout the remainder of my formalized education, whenever I caught myself talking to my friends in class, I would immediately stop. To this day when I am in church, in a seminar, or even at the movies, and the urge to talk comes over me, my hands start to cramp as I remember I will not talk in class, and I refocus on the sermon, speaker, or movie. Sometimes I wish the pastor, speaker, or theater owner would react directly to those who feel free to disrupt the concentration of others and roll a chalk board down the aisle, hand the offender a new piece of chalk, and say, "When this is over, you owe us I will not talk in class 101 times."

Here are some of the finer points of this lesson:

First, the fact that you are doing the physical act of writing causes whatever you're writing to become part of you. It is written across your heart and emblazoned upon your spirit.

Second, *I will not talk in class* is specific, clear, and to the point. This is the objective for any goal. This type of short, precise goal is exactly what we must set for our selves in our real estate investing business. We must know exactly the amount of money we want to make. We must know exactly the time frame we are going to make it in. And we must know exactly the number of deals it is going to take to reach our goal. We both know that the exact number will change as we start buying properties because we will make more money on some deals and less on others, but we must have a specific number for the purpose of creating our goal. After thirty days we will revisit the goal and make any adjustments needed.

Third, *I will not talk in class* was written *repeatedly*. This is a very important aspect of goal setting. You should repeatedly write your goals down to reinforce your resolve.

Do not misunderstand: this is not your daily planner or your "To Do" list. You need to repeatedly rewrite your most important long-term goals. This rewriting process has the same effect as *I will not talk in class*. The rewriting ingrains the goals in your conscious and sub-conscious mind. It makes them part of your living spirit. For me writing this book was one of those goals. Whenever I found myself getting off track, the small inner voice of my subconscious mind would remind me that I wasn't moving in the direction of my goals. Just as Ms. Simpson's lesson came back to me through the years whenever I was talking inappropriately, continually rewriting your most important long-term goals will keep you on track. As you start to wander off into meaningless time wasters, you'll find the goals magically popping into your head to remind you of things that are more important.

Faithfully, prayerfully, you have accepted the importance of writing down specific goals for your real estate business: the amount of money you want to make and the time frame you want to make it in. Don't forget to add the magic by rewriting these long-term goals regularly. Next we will discuss how we translate the amount of money we want to make and our time frame into the number of houses we have to sell or deals we have to do to reach our goal.

PITFALL: DO I HAVE TO CREATE A PLAN?

The creation of a simple plan is the second area that most people fail in. Even if you have your goals written down, if you don't create a plan for their implementation, you are wasting your time. Tell yourself now, "This is something I can do and I will not fail by overlooking these two simple exercises." We are in a simple business, not an easy business, but a simple business.

Don't Dismiss the Simple Stuff

This reminds me of the camping trip the legendary detective Sherlock Holmes and his sidekick, Dr. Watson, took in the English countryside. As darkness approached on the first evening, Sherlock Holmes and Watson settled into their respective sleeping bags.

Holmes asked Watson, "Tell me, Watson, what do you see?" "Ah," replied Watson, "I see a black velvet sky covered with bright stars and a full moon." Holmes inquired further, "So what does that say to you Watson?" "Well, Holmes, meteorologically speaking, it tells me that we are going to have a gorgeous day tomorrow." "Good observation, what else does it tell you?" "Holmes, astrologically it tells me that there are millions and millions of stars and therefore, millions and millions of universes." "Good work, Watson, what else does it say to you?" "Now wait a minute. Holmes, as we lie here gazing at these countless stars on this beautiful night, what does it say to *you?*" Holmes replied, "Someone stole our tent." It may take a few more pages before some of you "get" it. Please do not overlook the obvious.

MINDSET OF A MILLIONAIRE

In order to be successful, you must make the commitment. You must write down specific, measurable, time-based goals. Commit to your Real Estate Investment Goals now. Write them down every day starting now.

I will make $_____

in the next 120 days

through my real estate investments.

I will need to sell _____ houses at an estimated _____ profit to make this goal.

I will need to talk to _____ callers a day to make my sales.

FIGURE 2-1

Determine Your Real Estate Financial Goals

First, we need to determine the price of the average starter home in your area. For sake of this book we'll use $100,000; you will need to adjust for your area. Suppose you want to acquire a million dollars worth of property over the next 120 days. The math is pretty basic: $1,000,000 worth of property divided by the cost of the average starter home of $100,000 means you must purchase ten homes in the next four months.

For those of you who are novice investors or inactive investors, this may seem like a daunting task. For those of us who are actively in the business, this is a snap. It is only two-and-a-half homes per month or one house every twelve days. Now if—as some gurus teach—you had to go to the classified section of your local newspaper to find sellers who might be offering an attractive price, this would be a very arduous task. I'm not going to ask you to call the numbers in the ads in the newspaper. I've done that and it's the quickest way for your self-image to take a severe beating. Not to worry—in Chapter 3 we will cover nine Surefire Methods to have motivated sellers calling you. Until you start your business, you'll have to take my word for some of the numbers I'm sharing with you now. Even as a beginner you will learn how to close one deal for every thirty to thirty-five callers to your business. Please note that I said callers *to* you. More on this later.

As you gain a little experience, your closing ratio will go up. You need to buy one $100,000 property every twelve days to meet your goal. You also need to have about thirty to thirty-five conversations to close one deal. To be on the safe side, let's push the number of callers to fifty.

To talk to fifty sellers over a twelve-day period, we need to talk to a whopping 4.17 sellers per day. Using the nine Surefire Methods in

Chapter 3, it's easy to have motivated sellers calling you, and 4.17 is a very attainable number. Don't worry, you're not going to have to quit your job to take these calls. I'll teach you how to have your business put on autopilot. You'll still have plenty to do, but the busywork that eats up so much time will be farmed out. Now that you have your financial goals established and written down: the amount of money you want to make, the number of houses you have to sell in the next 120 days to make that happen, the number of calls you need to receive, and the number of people you need to talk to in a day. Now that you know how many sellers you need to have call you, you can get started with your business.

Equipment Checklist

Before you begin, you should make sure that you have the necessary equipment. There are a few things you are going to need:

- **A phone.** I bet you already own more than one.

- **A fax.** Most homes in America today have a fax. Don't sweat it if you don't; most local office supply stores sell them for less than $200.

- **Business cards.** I'm not talking about the kind of cards you see the local real estate agent use, cards with their picture and basic contact information. I'm talking about a card that creates business by telling the benefits you can offer to a seller. Appendix D on page 244 is a copy of the card I use. It's doublesided and folds over. It came to me from a very savvy marketer and successful real estate investor in Colorado, Richard Roop. Most American businesses miss an excellent opportunity to sell their company—using business cards as a sales brochure. You can make a photo-copy of this card and take it to your local Kinko's and have yours ready in less than forty-eight hours. The key to these cards (and believe me, it was the hardest thing for me to get used to) is the color. They must be an obnoxious neon green. You'll hate these cards; in fact they may even be an embarrassment to you *until* you buy a house because of your cards *and* turn a profit of $20,000 or more. Then you'll love these cards as much as I do, and you will be giving them to everyone you meet.

Chapter Summary

1. The secret behind "I will not talk in class": *Write it down.*

2. You've committed to creating your goals and writing them down. You have committed to writing them down, right?

3. You have agreed to add the "magic" to your goals process by rewriting them regularly.

4. You've learned *not* to let someone steal your tent by over-looking the obvious. (Please reread items 1 through 3.)

5. Set up your office by purchasing the proper equipment.

You now know the formula for breaking into the first phase of being a millionaire. There is much more later on about the three phases of becoming a millionaire, what they are and how to break through each level.

In the next chapter we will cover the "Nine Surefire Methods To Get Motivated Sellers Calling You."

Pitfalls Recap

I DON'T HAVE TO WRITE THEM DOWN. Written goals are a must for you to reach your maximum level of success. Take the time to create a Top 10 goals sheet for your life and your business. Make each goal as clear as possible: Be concise and be specific.

DO I HAVE TO CREATE A WRITTEN PLAN? Plan for your success by knowing exactly how many houses you must buy and how much profit you need per transaction to fulfill your plan. Keep your plan handy as you will refine the techniques used for its attainment daily.

Don't let someone steal your tent by overlooking the obvious.

I BOUGHT THE BOOK.
WHAT DO I DO NOW?

YOUR FIRST THIRTY days as a real estate investor may be the single most important time in your financial life. Abraham Lincoln once said, "If I had eight hours to chop down a tree, I would spend seven hours sharpening my ax." Your first thirty days is your "ax-sharpening" period. Many of you will worry if you haven't completed your first deal in the next thirty days. Take a deep breath—you're going to be just fine.

This is a numbers game. Any time you are dealing with the public and it involves buying and selling it is simply a numbers game. Robert Allen ask his students to make one hundred written offers before they decide whether or not this business is for them. The reason he asks for one hundred written offers is simple: No matter how bad you are at this, someone is going to say yes out of a hundred serious written offers.

Ron LeGrand tells his students, "Just go out and make a mess; you can't screw things up enough to keep from making money in this business as long as you're making enough offers." There is a lot of business savvy and common sense in both of those statements.

In this chapter we are going to cover the nine surefire ways to have motivated sellers calling you. Your phone ringing is the best way for you to fill your deal pipeline. A full deal pipeline is how you can make enough offers to get your first deal done. It's your first deal that will be the most difficult, so let's get you through it and the rest will be downhill. Remember: It's all a numbers game.

Method 1: Signs

In my experience the number-one way to get motivated sellers calling you is to use signs. You have probably seen these signs in your area. They read:

WE BUY HOUSES
CA$H
(817) 555–1212

There is a reason these signs dominate the creative real estate business: They work. You've seen them along the side of the road and stuck on telephone poles. You've probably seen them at busy intersections. Those are all good places to get your signs out and to get your phone ringing.

If you are new to the business, you will probably order your signs and think, "Hey, here's an area I could save a little money in. I'll put the signs out myself." Its exactly what I thought when I got started. In fact, I ordered my first hundred signs and anxiously awaited their arrival. As soon as they came in, I rushed over to the local home improvement store and went straight to the lumber department. I bought a hundred wooden stakes. They look like props from one of those B-grade vampire films of the fifties and sixties. They're approximately three feet long with one end cut to a sharp point. They cost about a dollar each.

Personally, I thought the vampire analogy was excellent because I pictured myself driving a stake through the heart of the competition. But of course, I was new to the business and had not realized this one simple pitfall.

PITFALL: YOU DON'T HAVE TO BE THE BIG DOG TO GET RICH IN THIS BUSINESS

This is a business in which it is very easy to let negative thinking steal your fortune right from under your nose. If you are not careful with your thinking, you'll start to see other investors' signs everywhere and feel as if there are no deals left for you. Or you start to think you got into the game too late. It's always been that way with me—a day late and a dollar short.

STOP IT. ENOUGH ALREADY.

You started to get me down just writing all those lies. Very early on in my investing career, I had those same down-in-the-mouth thoughts. I was so worried because there were so many investors in my area, and I thought all the deals would be gone before I could even get started. I have some very sage advice that I will pass along to you now. Is there a tall building where you live? Take your significant other to dinner there one night soon. Enjoy a romantic evening out on the town with good food and wine—you know the kind of night I'm talking about. It's the kind of night where for a very brief moment you know how the other side lives. While you're reveling in the atmosphere, take your significant other by the hand and walk over to the window. Look out at all of those lights out there, millions and millions of lights, so many lights they look like the stars in the heavens. As you gaze into the night, concentrate on this one thought: EACH YEAR ONLY FIFTEEN OF THOSE PEOPLE OUT THERE HAVE TO SAY "YES" TO MAKE ME RICH.

So, get over it and go out and do some business.

With my wooden stakes in hand, I went to the roofing supplies store and purchased a box of roofing nails. Roofing nails are the ones with what appears to be a large washer slipped over the nail. These looked as if they would work just fine for nailing my signs to the wooden stakes. I got home, nailed my signs together, loaded them into the back of my Mercedes and announced, "Honey, I'm going to go put our signs out." After about ten signs I picked up my cell phone and announced, "Honey, I'm coming home." It stank. It was not what I envisioned a successful real estate investor doing. There has to be a better way, and there is.

There are people putting out signs on a regular basis—you just have to hire them. If you look in the yellow pages under sign placement there aren't any listings, not even a category using the name. If you call the regular sign companies to see which ones place signs, you won't have any luck either. In fact, when I did this they acted as if I had just woken up from a deep sleep because I must have been dreaming if I thought they would actually put the signs out for me.

OK, it's time to think this thing through. I see signs out every weekend advertising new subdivisions. Who puts these signs out? Well, there's always one way to find out—ask. I went to three new subdivisions before I got the answer I needed. Here's what I did: I went into the model home/sales office of the new subdivision and asked for the sales manager. If the sales manager was on duty, I would simply ask him or her who put their signs out. The first two looked at me as if they were a dog that had just heard a strange high-pitched sound—the look a dog gives you when it turns its head from side to side with that lost-in-space expression. But the third was actually from this planet and knew immediately who to put me in touch with. I called and discovered there were only three companies in town that did this type of work. All three of them worked exclusively for builders. This explains why I couldn't just look them up in the yellow pages. It is such a small niche that the only way they advertise is by word of mouth. As I learned more about their business and the way they operated, I was shocked to see what a specialized and highly efficient system they had developed. These sign placement companies use heavy-duty pickup trucks that pull specially designed trailers carrying a few hundred signs at one time. There are normally two or three workers going out on a sign run, and they spend more time driving to the location than they do putting the signs out.

One of the great benefits to having these companies put your signs out is that they will be aware of all of the city or county regulations regarding signs. For example, in my area, signs of this nature can only be put out after 3:00 P.M. on Friday and must be picked up by midnight on Sunday. The fines for violating this law can add up rather quickly. One of the areas where I do a lot of my business requires a permit for each sign put out. At $150 per permit, it doesn't make sense to spend that kind of money. I have the placement company go right up to this city's borders with my signs. That way I still get a lot of benefit without paying the permit fee. All of this is too much to keep track of, so let the professionals do their job and go do some more deals.

The cost for sign placement varies wildly across the country. I've seen as low as fifty cents per sign per weekend and as high as three dollars per sign per weekend. Whatever the cost is in your area, please remember that the average profit off one deal is $25,000. How many deals do you have to do to cover your sign marketing costs for a full year?

If you need a place to look at signs or to buy your signs, go to the SIGNAGE link at http://www.AreYouDUMBEnoughToBeRICH.com.

Method 2: Builders

This method is placed in the number-two spot not because it is the second most successful method, but because it is so closely aligned with Method 1. When you are in the Model Home/Sales Office of the new subdivisions looking for sign placement companies and talking to the sales manager, you can accomplish a nice bit of marketing as well.

Picture this if you will: It's a typical Sunday afternoon, and all over America couples are going out for a Sunday drive. Many of these couples will end up driving through a new subdivision just to see what's going on and to dream a little bit. They will see some homes that pique their interest, and they will pull the car over just to take a quick look inside. What harm could looking do, right? Once they are inside, the smell of newness sweeps over them like a powerful aphrodisiac. So the conversation changes to, "Why don't we stop in the Sales Office and just see what these homes are selling for and what the payments would be. Just for informational purposes." Once in the Sales Office, the couple learns about all the super incentives the builder is throwing in to get these last few homes sold.

They hear about all of the easy ways to qualify for financing available through the builder. The couple wants to investigate buying a new home more, but they have this one nagging problem: They have to sell their old home first. This is where you come in. While you are talking to the sales manager about signs, make sure you leave an ample supply of your business cards. Tell the sales manager to give prospective new home buyers your card if they haven't sold their old house yet. This helps attract more motivated sellers, so you can pick up a few extra deals a year.

Method 3: Cards

As pointed out in Chapter 2, a good business card is a vital marketing device for you and your company. Card proliferation is another way to pick up two or three extra deals a year. Make sure everyone you come in contact with gets one of your cards. You never know who they are going to pass your card along to or when their personal situation will change.

Method 4: Flyers

Flyers can be a very inexpensive way to get you message out. All you have to do is blanket a neighborhood where you want to buy property. The "We Buy Houses Cash" flyer carries the constant "We Buy Houses" marketing message to your prospects and will pick you up a few more deals per year. Please note, this is not something you can do once and expect to get great results. If you find a neighborhood where you want to buy property, I suggest you blanket that neighborhood every six weeks with your flyer. Flyers are going to cost you around a dime each, and it should cost you no more than a dime to get them delivered. How do you find someone to put your flyers out? Well, there's no magic here: I found mine by seeing a guy walking through the neighborhood putting flyers out.

Method 5: Classifieds

In most markets, you can purchase a three-line classified for only a few dollars a week. The classified will carry the same message as your flyers, business cards, and signs:

WE BUY HOUSES
CA$H
(817) 555–1212

One of my investor friends named Bill has all of his marketing material read a little more personally with "Bill Buys Houses." Either way, the message is the same and the results will come. Please remember there are no methods here that will cause your phone to be flooded with deals. Each of these methods will generate enough calls to get you a few deals per year. A few deals here, a few deals there, and suddenly you have a booming business.

Method 6: Direct Mail

One of the oldest forms of inexpensive marketing is direct mail. When you use direct mail, be sure to adhere to a few basic success rules. For example, take the pre-foreclosure letter found at http://www.AreYouDUMBEnoughToBeRICH.com by clicking on the "In Foreclosure?" menu button. If you use this form, make sure you have someone hand-address your envelopes. Yes, hand-address. This small act will multiply the number of responses you receive. The pre-foreclosure letter generates a response rate of approximately 3 percent. If you know anything about direct mail, you know that 3 percent is huge. The reason the response rate is so high is the quality of the list. We'll go more in detail about this in Chapters 9 and 10.

Always put a real stamp on the letter. What you are trying to achieve is the look of a single letter mailed out to a prospective seller. I also do not use mailing labels for my return address. The letter arrives in a completely handwritten envelope with a real stamp on it. It looks like a personal letter from a friend, and it could very well end up being just that.

Method 7: Web Site

This is the least expensive way possible to let people know you are in the real estate business as an investor. It is such a great method I have devoted an entire chapter, Chapter 15, to real estate on the Web. There are too many aspects of this to try to explain it to you here. There is more coming, lots more.

Method 8: Networking

In the first chapter I told you about real estate investment clubs and how to find the one in your area, even how to get the information to start one if there isn't one in your area. This is a vital method of networking. Become a member and meet others who are doing the same thing. Civic organizations are another way to get the word out. As you become more adept at the business, you can actually be a guest speaker at these clubs and start spreading the word like wildfire. You might give a short presentation on helping people prevent foreclosure and what that could mean to their credit report. There are many great topics you could present as you start doing a few deals, and believe me, the program chairs for those clubs are looking for speakers left and right.

Method 9: Realtors, Real Estate Agents, and Brokers

I purposefully put this method last because it is the last way I want you to use to start filling your pipeline with motivated sellers. Most people who fall into one of these three headings will not want to do business with you. You do not fit into their idea of the real estate business. They are wearing blinders and can only see as far as their next commission check. There are a few, and I stress a few, who can see the ability for the traditional real estate world and the nontraditional world to live together profitably, but there are only a few. Once you find one or two Realtors, real estate agents, or brokers who are willing to work with you, they will be worth their weight in gold. You'll want to put them on your Christmas card list. Again, we'll go into detail about how you find these team members in Chapter 21.

Chapter Summary

In the first thirty days of your real estate career you need to set everything up and get your name out. Use as many of the nine surefire ways to get customers as possible. No single one will bring in as many customers as you need, but used in combination, these methods will put you on the road to riches.

In the next chapter we're going to learn what to say to these prospective sellers when they call so we can start filling the pipeline.

Pitfalls Recap

YOU DON'T HAVE TO BE THE BIG DOG TO GET RICH IN THIS BUSINESS.
Please remember, it only takes a few deals a year to completely change your financial future.

WOW!

"WOW" WILL become one of the most important words in your real estate investing career. As we go forward you will read several times, *This is not an easy business, but it is a simple business.* Learn the WOW system and it will help you keep your business simple.

WOW is an acronym to remind you to gather all the information you need from the sellers while you have them on the phone.

The first thing you must do is *remember* to use the WOW system. I want you to commit to memory the following sentence: *"To make money in real estate you have to WOW me!"*

Your phone has likely started to ring from the myriad of low-cost marketing items you've applied from Chapter 3. You need to be prepared to ask the seller about their property. Be assured, if you ask the seller to tell you about their *home,* you're in for a long conversation and it will take you ten minutes or more to get back to business.

Please note that anytime I am speaking with a prospective seller, the home is always referred to as "the property" or simply "the house." I do this to remove any emotional attachment the seller may have with the home. When I am selling a property, however, I always refer to it as a "home."

Remember, at this stage of the game you shouldn't be concerned if there is a new Berber carpet in the master bedroom. You want to know the financial details. If those details WOW you, then you'll be deeply interested in the carpet in the master bedroom along with all of the other unique details concerning the property.

The easiest way for you to remember the WOW system and how to use it is to place a spiral notebook next to your phone and only use it for real estate conversations. When a prospective seller calls, go to a clean sheet of paper and write the word WOW in big letters vertically down the page. Or you can use the form in Figure 4.1.

Worth

The first "W" stands for *worth.* Commit this question to memory.

"Mr./Ms. Seller, if I were to have your home appraised today, what would it appraise for?" Most sellers have a pretty good idea of what their home is worth.

It will not always be on the money, but normally it will be close enough for you to work with at this point in the deal. When they answer, simply write the number next to the first W on your page. Then ask, "How did you come up with that number?" Pay close attention here as there may be several clues hidden in their answer that tell you this is a good deal. One of these clues would be the

---

WOW FORM

1. Worth: What would your property be appraised for today?

How did you come up with that number?

2. Owe: What do you owe on the property?

Would you take what you owe for the property?

How much are your payments?

Are the payments P.I.T.I. (Principal, Interest, Taxes, and Insurance)?

Are the taxes and the insurance escrowed? If not, are they paid?

Are you paid through the end of the month?

3. Want: What do you want to get out of this sale?

Are you telling me, if I don't pay you X for this property then we can't do business?

OK, Mr./Ms. _____, let me put a pencil to these numbers and see if I can come up with something that will make sense for both of us. I'll give you a call in the morning. Where can I reach you?

FIGURE 4-1

answer, "That's what the tax appraisal is." If the seller is relying on a tax appraisal, this could be an excellent prospect because most tax appraisals are low.

PITFALL: DO NOT GET LAZY WHEN IT COMES TO TAX APPRAISALS

I've worked with many investors from all over the country and I can't tell you how many of them I've seen get into financial trouble because they used the tax appraisal as the market value for the property. Don't become another sad statistic. Only base your buying decisions on the value established for the property through comparable sales (comps). I'll go into comps in Chapter 6 and tell you the best way to get solid comps, but for now let's stick with the WOW technique.

Another answer you will hear is, "Because that's how much I've got in it." If you are in a rapidly appreciating area this could be a gold-mine, otherwise it probably has no bearing on reality. Be sure to make a note of the prospective seller's answer next to the number they give you.

Owe

The "O" in WOW stands for *owe*. The second question is, "What do you owe on the property?" As I teach all over the country. I have students ask, "Won't they just tell me its none of my business?" Yes, sometimes you will hear that, but you'll only hear it from a nonmotivated seller. If the seller is unwilling to give you this vital piece of information, there is no deal here. If he or she refuses to answer this question you should say, "All I'm trying to do is get enough information to properly evaluate whether this is a deal we can make work for both of us." At that point, if the seller is still unwilling to give you the information, politely get off the phone by saying, "I understand that you feel uncomfortable right now about sharing that information with me. Please keep my name and phone number, and if you don't sell your home in the next few weeks give me a call."

You'll discover that having a home sit on the market a few extra weeks or months will loosen a seller's tongue quite a bit. After making a few additional payments, it will suddenly become very clear to this type of seller that it *is* your business.

Why is it important that we know how much is owed on the underlying loan? You cannot accurately construct your offers (yes plural, more about multiple offers in Chapter 13) for the property without a loan balance. Please note that all we need at this point is an approximate balance on the mortgage. Then ask, "How much are your payments?" After you have gotten this information be sure to ask the seller whether the payment is P.I.T.I.

P.I.T.I. is a term used in the industry that stands for *Principle, Interest, Taxes, and Insurance.* It's an all-inclusive number. By asking this question, you are ensuring yourself that there aren't any surprises lurking out there regarding back taxes.

PITFALL: FORGETTING THE DIFFERENCE BETWEEN CURRENT AND PAID

You must be in the habit of asking pointed questions that require a yes or no response and have as little room as humanly possible for misinterpretation. If you don't, you could get an expensive lesson in the school of hard knocks like I did. I had purchased a very nice home, over 5,000 square feet in a very nice subdivision. In fact the owners paid me to take their house (Chapter 12 is devoted to this incredibly powerful buying technique).

As you should do on any property you are considering purchasing, I called my title company and asked them to do a "quick look," sometimes called an O & F (owners and encumbrances), at the title to see if there were any other liens outstanding on the property.

The title company responded that there were first and second mortgages and that the taxes and insurance were current. I purchased the property and started moving forward with aggressive marketing of the home. Several weeks later I received a past due statement concerning the property taxes. Thinking this was simply an error, I called the county appraisers office only to discover the taxes had not been paid. How did this happen? Is the title company at fault here? Did I have to pay those taxes? Let's start with the last question first.

Yes, I had to pay the taxes, to the tune of approximately $10,000. Sure, I could have backed out of the deal at that point, but there was enough equity for me to still want the home.

The property taxes had fallen during a gap of time where technically they were current when I asked the question, but still had not been paid. In Texas the taxes are assessed during a certain month—October for us. After assessment there may be two months, three months, or longer for the homeowner to the pay the taxes before they are considered late. If the homeowner had put a down payment of 20 percent or more on the property when he purchased the home, in most cases it would now become the homeowner's decision whether or not to have taxes and insurance escrowed. It is a much less expensive choice to pay your taxes and insurance separately, but not everyone has the luxury of being able to pay 20 percent down.

This particular home fell in the gap of time described above. Since the taxes had been assessed but had not yet become late, they were technically current. Most states agree with this definition of current and late. The bottom line was that I had to pay almost $10,000 in back taxes. Obviously I changed the way I did business from that point forward. Here is what I want to make sure you are doing to prevent this from happening to you:

As you are going through the WOW questions, ask the homeowner if the taxes and insurance are escrowed. If they are, great don't worry about it and continue to gather the needed information. If they are not escrowed, you want to ask the homeowner whether they are *paid.* This is very important.

The difference between taxes being *paid* and being *current* could be $10,000 as it was for me. By asking if the taxes are paid, you are much less likely to be surprised. Please go one step further by asking the question again, but this time ask it differently: "So what you're telling me is that the taxes have been paid through the end of last month?" This becomes a very pointed question and prevents any $10,000.00 surprises from popping up on you.

Want

The third letter in WOW stands for *want*. Ask the seller, "What do you want to get out of this sale?" The first response is likely to be whatever the full asking price of the property is. Then follow up by asking, "Are you telling me, if I don't pay you X for this property, then we can't do business?" If the answer comes back "Yes, that's what I'm telling you," then you are not dealing with a motivated seller and it's time to get off the phone. Many times the reply will be something like, "Well no, I'm not saying that." If this is the response, continue by saying something like this: "All right, Mr./Ms. Seller, you said you owe $140,000 on the property, and you're asking $195,000. Would you take what you owe for the property?" This may seem like an absurd question, but you could be surprised by the answer to this question. Granted, it will be in a very small percentage of cases, but the occasional *yes* will put many thousands of dollars of CA$H in your pocket. It has much better odds than playing Lotto.

Many sellers are looking for debt relief. Of course they will take extra cash if they can get it, but in many cases they're really just looking for an out. Their dream home has become a nightmare.

Wrapping Up the Phone Call

What we are trying to determine here is the seller's true motivation. Sellers might not always tell you the truth if you ask why they are selling their home. These questions are designed to get past the surface answer and uncover the real reason for the sale.

After we have received an answer to all three of the WOW questions it's time to politely get off the phone. This is a good idea because you need to do some homework before deciding whether you are interested. You can easily end this conversation by saying, "OK, Mr./Ms. Seller, let me put a pencil to these numbers and see if

I can come up with something that will make sense for both of us. I'll give you a call in the morning. Where can I reach you?"

Chapter Summary

By now you should have people calling you up interested in selling you their homes. Before you go ahead and buy a property, you need to make sure it's worth your while. Use the WOW system to gather all the needed information to make multiple offers.

In Chapter 13, I'll show you a simple method for creating these multiple offers where we can let the sellers decide what works best for them. Any choice they pick will be a Win/Win situation for us.

Pitfalls Recap

DO NOT GET LAZY WHEN IT COMES TO TAX APPRAISALS. Only base your buying decisions on the value established for the property through comparable sales (comps).

FORGETTING THE DIFFERENCE BETWEEN CURRENT AND PAID. On a property where the taxes are not escrowed always make sure the taxes are *paid* and not simply current. Please remember there is a difference and that difference could save you or cost you $10,000.00 or more.

FINDING INVESTORS

COME ON IN, THE INVESTOR
POOL IS FINE

"CASH! CASH! I've got to have some cash put together before I can buy any properties. I don't have any. I don't know where to get it. Oh, what shall I do, what shall I do?" This agonizing cry echoes through the halls of meeting rooms across America, as I travel teaching investors to stop outsmarting themselves and learn to be Dumb Enough to Be Rich.

As a new real estate investor, the idea of quickly and easily putting your hands on literally hundreds of thousands of dollars of investment capital seems like a pipe dream. Who would be crazy enough to give you that kind of money? One reason it sounds so crazy is because it hasn't happened to you yet. Once you master this easy system of finding money you'll never want for funds to buy property with again.

What I'm going to share with you now has been built over the last seventeen plus years and has been responsible for generating a few million dollars worth of investment capital. Not all of these funds were used in real estate, but they were all raised using this simple system.

You might think that once you start making all of this money you should invest in your own deals and save the interest on any funds you might have had to borrow, right? Wrong. Hold the book up close to your eyes. I don't want everyone else to see this:

I don't put my money in real estate deals.

Quick, we better burn this book; he's starting to talk heresy and sacrilege now. I put my money into government-guaranteed investments earning me 20 plus percent. In subsequent chapters I'll explain the specific areas I invest in and how you can too. There are two investments I make, and each one has its own chapter detailing what it is and how you can get into it yourself.

Let me tell you why you shouldn't put your own money into real estate deals. If you have the ability to easily and quickly raise hundreds of thousands, even millions, of dollars to do your deals at a rate of 12 to 15 percent (at the time of this writing) and if you can make more than 20 percent guaranteed by the government, doesn't it make sense to do just that?

PITFALL: PARTNERS—THE BIG LIE

Remember the pitfall from the Introduction: Beware of Partners. Through the years I've seen many—and have unfortunately been involved in a few—partnerships that sounded great on the front end and were not so great on the back end. Does this sound familiar: "You put up the money, I'll do the work, and we'll split the profits."? What's the reason I refer to this as "The Big Lie"? We have been taught—programmed is more like it—to think this is a good deal. If we pay 3 to 5 points on borrowed funds and interest as high as 15 percent, at the time of this writing, we think of that as very expensive, yet we easily jump into a partnership and even feel a debt of gratitude to the investor for making this great opportunity available to us. Let's take a look at what the financial numbers really are.

I'll use a real-life house and a couple of imaginary investor scenarios as an example. I purchased a rehabber for $50,000 that needed extensive work to the tune of $30,000. This property would have sold for $135,000 to an all-cash buyer and did sell for $149,900 because I offered seller financing. The profit range is between $55,000 from the all-cash buyer to $70,000 using owner financing. Under either profit scenario our cash needs are going to total $80,000 ($50,000 to purchase + $30,000 to rehab).

By using our partner to put up the money and subsequently splitting the profits, we will end up with our final profit range of $27,500 to $35,000, half of the above-mentioned profit.

By using what may appear to be more costly funds from a hard-money lender (more on this later) or from my personal favorite, a private investor, our final profit range is $40,000 to $55,000.

> If we are paying 5 points up front, our points will cost us $4,000 ($80,000 borrowed X 5 points or percent = $4,000). Should it take us a full six months to rehab and then sell the property, we will be charged 15 percent interest on the $80,000 for six months, which equals $6,000. Now add our two money costs together: 5 points is $4,000 plus 15 percent interest on $80,000 for six months is $6,000 for a grand total of $10,000 of interest or money cost.
>
> By paying for hard money or using a private investor we are able to increase our profit range by $12,500 to $20,000.

OK, I am convinced I can get money much cheaper if I can borrow it, but how do I find this wellspring of cash? Using a script is the best way I know of to raise lots and lots of money. This surprisingly simple method will allow you to find all of the money you will ever need to do real estate deals with.

Please promise me you will not change this script until you have used it for at least thirty days as it is. If you adhere to this, you'll discover that it works. It is simple and deceptively powerful. Here it is.

> I know this is not for you, but who do you know that might be interested in earning 12 to 15 percent on their money, secured by a first lien on real estate, short-term, 6 to 12 months?

Did you have to reread the entire paragraph because you thought something had surely been left out? Most of my students have a hard time accepting this fact, it is just that simple. Well, accept it.

FINDING AN INVESTOR WORKSHEET

Potential Investor's Name: _____

_____

_____

Phone Number: _____

Contact Information: _____

_____

_____

_____

Date: _____

I know this is not for you, but who do you know that might be interested in earning 12 to 15 percent on their money, secured by a first lien on real estate, short-term, 6 to 12 months?

Response: _____

_____

_____

_____

Details of Property Involved: _____

_____

_____

_____

_____

FIGURE 5-1

Robert Allen and Mark Victor Hansen, in their best-selling book *The One Minute Millionaire* relay one of the theories of fourteenth-century English philosopher William of Occam. The theory, called "Occam's Razor" after its creator, states, "The best solution to a problem is almost always the simplest solution." All over the country students ask again and again, "Can it be that simple?" and again and again all over the country I tell them that it is.

PITFALL: IT'S NOT THAT EASY

Yes it is. Put your confidence in the script on raising money. It is just that simple. Don't mess it up. Learn the script word for word and use it exactly the way it is written.

Why is this script so powerful? Let's break it down and examine each of its core components.

First the phrase, *I know this is not for you.* Why would I talk to someone about money if I know this is not for you? This phrase takes all of the pressure and stress off you and the person you are speaking with. If I state up front, *I know this is not for you,* then neither of us has to feel the least bit uncomfortable moving forward with the conversation. That's all it is at this point; a conversation. I am not trying to sell him anything and he does not have to turn me down because I'm not asking him to invest. I've told him that with the simple phrase, *I know this is not for you.* This phrase will give you the confidence to speak with ease about investment money. Remember, *I know this is not for you* so anything you tell me, Mr./Ms. Prospective Investor is OK.

As my dad taught me growing up, "If you don't ask you don't get. Besides, what's the worst thing anybody can say to you? No? I don't know anybody that's ever been killed by a No." It took me many years to fully understand the power of that statement. My dad always had a knack for creating cash through selling. Now I know why: He understood the power of simply asking the question.

PITFALL: PREJUDGING

One of the ultimate sins of the real estate business is pre-judging. Unless your name is "The Amazing Kreskin" or you too have the ability to read someone's mind, do *not* pretend to know what the other person is thinking, what is best for them, or how much money they have. These assumptions will be extremely costly to you. They will shorten your career, especially when you are dealing with raising investment capital. This is not the only time in the book I will tell you not to prejudge people.

The second phrase, "but who do you know," is a quietly powerful question. The psychology going on here is purely subconscious. We have subconsciously challenged their ego for the second time in the last twelve words. Did you catch that? The first subconscious challenge came when we stated, "I know this is not for you." Now we are subconsciously challenging the content and quality of their contact base with "but who do you know."

In the world of selling it's called the "Take-Away Close." We are subconsciously taking the potential investment we are offering away from them. Of course, any time someone is taking something away from us, we immediately want it more. Now we have not only taken it away from them with the statement *"I know this is not for you"* but we have offered it to someone else with the question *"but who do you know."* The question implies we aren't going to let them have it but we will let someone they know have it.

Now we start getting into the meat of the script. The next section of the question, *"that might be interested"* is another no-pressure phrase. We aren't asking if they know somebody that *would* be interested, only if they know somebody that *might* be interested. Again we are allowing for this to happen in a very conversational, nonconfrontational, easygoing style.

If you like a challenge, we have now taken the Take-Away Close one step further. First we took it away from the person we are talking with by saying, *"I know this is not for you."* We then subconsciously questioned their circle of influence by asking, *"but who do you know."* Now we subconsciously up the ante on questioning their circle of influence by saying, *"that might be interested."* The assumption here is that they may not even know of anybody *"that might be interested."*

Now for the hammer. We start to get into the world of the ridiculous here. Our next no-pressure phrase is *in earning 12 to 15 percent on their money.* I refer to this as the world of the ridiculous because as I am writing this, the current chairman of the Federal Reserve, Alan Greenspan, has cut the rate the Treasury charges banks for money yet again to a ridiculously low interest rate. The effect this has on our search for investors is terrific.

The certificate of deposit rates around the country are anywhere from 1.5 percent to 4 percent depending on the amount of time you are willing to tie your money up. Now here you come along and are asking *"but who do you know, that might be interested in earning 12 to 15 percent on their money?"* Sounds a little ridiculous doesn't it? Everyone would want to earn up to ten times more return on their investments than they are currently earning, right?

Now we are going to attack the investor's need for security by saying, *"secured by a first lien on real estate."* *Secured by a first lien on real estate* adds safety to this high rate of return we are offering. Many buying strategies have to do with "subject to" or "lease-purchase options," so how can we offer a first lien for the investor? It is really quite simple: If the investor requires a first lien position, all they have to do is write a bigger check.

By writing a check big enough to pay off the underlying first mortgage, our investor can take the first lien position. If the investor doesn't have enough money to cover the first lien and whatever additional funds we are going to need, then the investor will have to take a second lien position. You are likely to find the investors wanting the first lien position until they have completed a couple of transactions with you. Once you have proven yourself as a trustworthy steward of their money, the investor usually moves to the second lien position easily. The reason an investor would be willing to do this is the ability to increase the number of houses that can be bought and sold for the same investment. The more houses we can do with the same amount of invested money, the greater the amount of money both the investor and you can make.

The clinching statement and the last of our no-pressure phrases is, *"short-term, 6 to 12 months."* Think about what is running through the mind of the person you are talking to right about now.

He has been allowed to listen to what you have to say without having to have his defenses up because you said, *"I know this is not for you."* You haven't asked for money. You've only asked for a referral with the statement, *"but who do you know."*

You have taken any remnants of pressure out of the conversation with *"that might be interested."*

Now you have started to lay the pay off or benefits on the table with *"in earning 12 to 15 percent on their money."*

You added security to the mix with *"secured by a first lien on real estate."*

Then you wrapped up this powerful money-raising script with *"short-term, 6 to 12 months."* Investors are wary of investments requiring their money to be tied up for long periods of time.

In the nearly ten years I was in the financial services community, I was not only required to raise money myself, I also had to teach others how to do the same thing. In looking for the perfect investment for an investor, I taught students there several key benefits any investment must have. They are:

1. *Safety.* There are few things in the investment world more safe than a single-family home. The stock market certainly isn't one of them. One of the reasons it has been so easy to raise money using this script is the uncertainty of the stock market.

2. *Simplicity.* An investment has to be easily understood by the investor. What could be easier to understand than a single-family home?

3. *Return.* The amount of money the investor can make has to be appealing.

4. *Term.* The amount of time the investor's money is tied up cannot be too long. The shorter the term, the better.

5. *Ease of entry.* The investment must not require too great a sum of money or the investor will shy away.

Each of these benefits is easily accommodated by investing with us in single-family homes.

Chapter Summary

By using what may appear to be more costly funds from a hard-money lender or from a private investor, your profit range could be $55,000 to $70,000. Use the script to get them interested, and you will have all the money you'll ever need to do deals with.

Pitfalls Recap

PARTNERS—THE BIG LIE! Remember, don't get suckered in with the offer of, "I'll put up the money, you do the work and we'll split 50/50." There are plenty of hard-money investors and private investors you can deal with for a lot less money.

IT'S NOT THAT EASY! YES IT IS! Don't allow yourself to overcomplicate this business.

PREJUDGING. Never try to determine what is best for the seller or an investor. Play the numbers game by using the script with everyone you know.

BUYING HUDs

FINALLY I'M ON THE
GOVERNMENT PAYROLL

WHAT ARE HUD properties? And can you build your career on them? HUD stands for the U.S. Department of Housing and Urban Development, whose mission is to help Americans buy affordable homes. Part of their work involves insuring mortgages. When someone with a HUD-insured mortgage is unable to make their mortgage payments, the lender forecloses on the home. HUD will pay the lender the remainder of the mortgage and then takes over ownership of the property. HUD then attempts to sell the home as quickly as possible for market value. Because these homes are often sold at a discount, they can be a great investment.

To answer the second question, you do not want to try to build your career on HUD properties. HUD is an excellent way to purchase a few extra properties per year, but it is too unpredictable to build a career on. There are several factors preventing HUD from being a stable source for property. First, the supply tends to change radically based on the foreclosure rate in the country. As I am writing this, the foreclosure rate in America is steadily increasing. For real estate investors that's good news. Our business is not cyclical. When times are good in the traditional market, our market is good. When times are bad in the traditional market, our market is *red hot.*

Kris, my absolute angel of a wife, tells me sometimes I get just a little too happy when I see the foreclosure rate going up. Sometimes I get downright giddy. It's because I know that bigger checks are on the way and the speed with which they will arrive is increasing.

Getting Started

The first thing you want to do is familiarize yourself with the HUD inventory. The easiest way is to go to the HUD Web site located at www. HUD.org. Once you are at the site, simply click on your state. After doing this you will see a list of cities where HUD currently owns property. If a particular city isn't listed, keep checking; the inventory list is updated daily.

Now click on the cities you want to see properties in. This will pull up a current listing of all the properties available in the selected cities.

As you begin to review the available properties, you will see at the right side of each listing one of these phrases: Owner Occupant (with a bid date), Daily Owner Occupant, or Daily All Purchasers.

The first two categories are for people who are buying a home for their personal residence. Unless you are looking for a home for yourself, the Owner Occupant or the Daily Owner Occupant listings will do you no good at all.

PITFALL: BUYING A HUD HOUSE AS AN OWNER OCCUPANT

Do not attempt to purchase an Owner Occupant property as an investment thinking that the government will not find out about it. They will. Not only will they find out about it, they will not be in a very good mood when they do. It's wrong, so just don't do it.

Now print your list of properties in the cities that interest you. The next step is to take a yellow highlighter and mark the properties that are listed as Daily—All Purchasers. You are honing in on your possibilities.

When all of your possibilities have been highlighted, you move to the organizational phase of the HUD process. In this phase you are going to take a city atlas and locate the street address for each of the listed properties. This way you can quickly and easily lay out a property inspection route to go and see each property. The object here is to arrange your drive time in such a way that you are able to see as much property as possible in as little time as possible. The HUD Web site also contains a "Get A Map" button at the bottom of each listing. This works just as well as using an atlas. Personally I find it quicker to look them up myself in the city atlas.

Before you inspect these properties, you need to make arrangements to be able to get inside. One way to achieve this is to drag, kicking and screaming, a HUD-approved Realtor, real estate agent or broker to come along while you inspect the properties.

A better way of gaining access to HUD properties is to develop a close enough relationship with an agent or broker that he will give you a key of your own.

If you don't know the agent well, he will not likely give you a key.

Please remember this is their license and therefore their livelihood we are dealing with here. After you have developed a rapport and trust, you can ask for a key. This is a master key and will allow you to open all front doors in HUD houses in your community. You might look at six to ten properties in a normal day, so you'll want the ability to come and go as you please.

When you view the house, you need to quickly determine a ballpark estimate of any necessary repairs. There are several repair items that you need to become very familiar with as you research HUD properties.

There's nothing that puts a bigger smile on my face than seeing a HUD listing on the Internet stating "Foundation Repairs." Let me explain why my inner cash register starts to ring when I see "Foundation Repairs Needed." Most investors and almost all homeowners run from a home needing foundation repairs. That works totally in your favor. The only thing you need to do is locate a reputable foundation repair company. Look in the yellow pages when you have located a property needing foundation repairs. Call several of these companies and ask for a bid on the repairs. Be sure to tell the foundation company employee making the bid that you're an investor. Let them know that you will probably need work done on more than one house and will choose them in the future if they give you a good price.

At the time of this writing, in the Dallas/Fort Worth area I can get pier foundation repairs for less than $400 per pier, so foundation work is not that expensive. In different parts of the country these prices will vary, but you will likely be able to negotiate a good price. Remember to ask for a commercial discount. Let the inspector know that you will *not* be living in the house, that it will be resold. The resale of the property brings us to a very important pitfall.

PITFALL: FORGETTING THE LIFETIME TRANSFERABLE WARRANTY

Make absolutely sure that whoever is doing your repair work provides a Lifetime Transferable Warranty. This may be the most important part of their service. You want the repairs guaranteed for life so whoever you sell the property to will have confidence they aren't going to get stuck should the foundation resettle years from now. For your buyer to have that confidence, the Lifetime Warranty must be transferable and not only from you to your buyer but also from them to their buyer, should they ever decide to move. This means you have to ask the repairing company whether the warranty continues to be transferable by the new owners. A Lifetime Transferable Warranty is an excellent selling point when you are reselling the property.

Remember to get the Warranty Certificate from the company when the work is completed. Do not pay the invoice until you have the Warranty Certificate. This is very important.

Foundation repairs are just one of the many types of repairs you'll have the pleasure of becoming intimately familiar with when you decide to buy and sell HUD homes. I must warn you, your basic belief in mankind may be shaken when you start looking at HUD homes. Many of these properties are downright nasty. You'll find it hard to believe that families were actually living in these filthy conditions. The wonderful thing about HUD homes is that you can revive these properties to make them some of the nicest houses in the neighborhood. We're going to discuss, in much greater detail, many of the additional repairs common to HUD and in our industry in Chapters 7 and 8.

Now you must determine what you are willing to pay for the property. Please note, a good bid is not necessarily the winning bid. A good bid means you've done your homework and you've submitted your bid based on solid numbers. The first number you need to determine is the Blood, Sweat, and Tears Value.

STEPS TO BUYING A HUD HOME

1. Locate the HUD inventory on the Internet.

2. Create a list of the properties you want to look at.

3. Find a HUD Broker/Agent.

4. Lay out your viewing route in the most efficient order to look at these houses so that you can see the largest number possible in a single day.

5. Choose the properties you want to bid on.

6. Determine your bid.

7. Make a bid.

FIGURE 6-1

Determine the Blood, Sweat, and Tears Value

This simple formula will keep you out of trouble when bidding on HUD properties. The Blood, Sweat and Tears (BST) Value is the value of the property *after* the repairs and rehabilitation. It is what the property will sell for in its best cosmetic condition, after it has become a beautiful home.

The only surefire way to determine the BST Value is to work through a real estate agent/broker and have her gather the comps for you. This is a free service if you're doing business with the Realtor, real estate agent, or broker. The term "comps" is the shortened version of "comparable sales." It is what other properties have sold for in the same area within the last six months. This is not information you can get on the Internet. At the time of this writing there are several sites promoting their ability to provide current market values of property anywhere in the country for free. *They are not accurate.* I don't know about you, but when something has to do with my paycheck, I want it to be accurate down to the penny.

PITFALL: USING THE TAX-APPRAISED VALUE

Please do not allow yourself to take the easy way out on establishing the BST Value of a property. I repeat, you cannot get this information accurately over the Internet. Similarly, the property's tax appraisal is usually inaccurate as well. One of the biggest pitfalls you can run into is trying to use the property's tax-appraised value as a substitute for comps. Tax appraisals are rarely a true estimation of the property's market value because they are quickly outdated and don't always reflect additions to the house. Yes, the taxing authority may occasionally stumble upon the same number the comps provide, but understand it is a coincidence and not by design.

With your BST Value established you now need to multiply it by the HIP National Bank Deposit Factor, which is comprised of three very important components.

$$\text{HIP deposit factor} \ = \ \frac{\text{Contingency fee} +}{\text{profit margin} + \text{repairs}}$$

First is the "Uh-Oh Fee," which is the contingency fee. The Uh-Oh Fee or contingency fee helps to prevent any surprises from popping up that will cut into your profit on a property. Will there ever be any surprises on the properties you buy and sell? You bet there will be. Do you want to see my scars? Why do you think I call it the "Uh-Oh Fee"? The Uh-Oh Fee or contingency fee is 10 percent of the BST Value.

$$\text{Contingency fee} \ = \ .1 \ \times \ \text{BST}$$

The second component of the HIP National Bank Deposit Factor is the profit margin. It is my belief that you should never work for less than a 20 percent profit margin. Yes, that is 20 percent of the BST Value. Your time is worth at least 20 percent.

$$\text{Profit margin} \ = \ .2 \ \times \ \text{BST}$$

As a new investor, the concept of just how valuable your time is may be hard for you to accept. Please take my word on this one: As your investing career develops, you'll realize the true value of your time. When you do, you'll see that 20 percent is very fair.

The third ingredient of the HIP National Bank Deposit Factor is the estimate of the repairs that you did earlier.

Buying a HUD Property: An Example

We see a HUD-listed property and decide to inspect it personally. For the sake of this example, we are going to establish the HUD "As Is" or asking price at $151,000. After a conversation with our friendly neighborhood real estate agent/broker, we determine (through the use of comps) that the BST Value is $185,000.

DETERMINING THE BID ON A HUD HOME

Property Address: _____

_____

AS IS asking price: _____

BST number based on comps: _____

Contingency Fee (10% of BST):   _____

Profit Margin (20% of BST):   _____

Repairs (if needed):   _____

**HIP Deposit Factor (Contingency Fee +
Profit Margin + Repairs):**   _____

HUD Number (BST − HIP Deposit number):   _____

Maximum bid (HUD As Is Price × .82):   _____

If the HUD number is greater than the maximum bid, then it
should be a good deal, but be sure to bid the 82% number.

FIGURE 6-2

We now take the BST Value of $185,000 and apply the HIP National Bank Deposit Factors. First is our Uh-Oh Fee of 10 percent of BST; second is our profit margin of 20 percent of the BST; and last is our repairs component. For the sake of the example, we will establish the cost of repairs for this property to be $5,000.

Now our HUD Formula looks like this:

$$\text{HUD Number} = \frac{\text{BST} - \text{Uh-Oh fee} - \text{profit margin} - \text{repairs}}{}$$

BST Value (based on comps)	$185,000
Uh-Oh Fee (10 percent of BST)	− 18,500
Profit Margin (20 percent of BST)	− 37,000
Repairs	− <u>5,000</u>
HUD NUMBER	$124,500

With the HUD number established at $124,000 you must now compare it to the HUD "As Is" asking price for the property. The "As Is" price listed at the HUD Web site was $151,000. Next, you are now going to take 82 percent of the HUD "As Is" for your maximum bid.

Maximum bid $= .82 \times$ **AS IS Price**

Please note: HUD will *never* admit publicly to a willingness to accept 82 percent of their "As Is" value on a property. This comes from years of experience. The HUD "As Is" price of the property of $151,000 × .82 creates our maximum bid of $123,820.

At this point you want to compare our HUD number of $124,500 to the maximum bid of $123,820. The maximum bid number ($123,820) is lower than the HUD number of $124,500. Great. This now becomes a property you want to bid on. Your bid will be the 82 percent number of $123,820.

Good deal $=$ HUD number > Maximum bid

These numbers are not etched in stone, especially because they are based on estimates. However, these formulas will help keep you out of trouble by preventing you from overpaying for property.

After your maximum bid number is determined, contact your HUD-approved Realtor, real estate agent, or broker to place your bid with HUD.

Chapter Summary

HUD homes can be an excellent source of real estate. They are cheap and can be easily rehabilitated so that you can make a profit on your investment. Make sure you regularly check the HUD Web site for listings to make sure you don't miss out on a deal.

In the next two chapters we will go over how to best rehabilitate these homes without overdoing it.

Pitfalls Recap

BUYING A HUD HOUSE AS AN OWNER OCCUPANT. Never, under any circumstances should you try to buy an Owner Occupant HUD home if you aren't going to live in it. Uncle Sam refers to this as fraud and he tends to get pretty nasty about it.

FORGETTING THE LIFETIME TRANSFERABLE WARRANTY. When we are having the foundation on a property repaired, the most important factor may be the Lifetime Transferable Warranty. NEVER have foundation repairs done unless the repairing company can provide you with a Lifetime Transferable Warranty.

USING THE TAX-APPRAISED VALUE OF THE PROPERTY. Please don't be lazy! Remember the only true way to establish the market value of a property is through the use of comparable sales or comps.

GETTING TO THE
HEART OF REHAB?

ALL OF US should be recycling our trash to help the improve the environment and conserve our resources. If you're doing this already with your household trash, good for you. Maybe you should take a hard look at doing it with houses. There are few things in my life I've gotten more satisfaction from than taking an old, run-down house, the worst one in the subdivision, and making it like new, the nicest home in the neighborhood.

So how do we begin to rehabilitate a property? The first thing you have to do is build your "trash team." The trash team is the collection of subcontractors willing to help you revitalize this run-down property.

PITFALL: THE GENERAL CONTRACTOR/HANDYMAN TRAP

We've reached our first pitfall of the chapter in record time. You have to be extremely careful when hiring your subcontractors. If you do not watch your cash here, the subcontractors will be the ones making all the money. Do you want to see my scars?

The first thing I personally look for in a subcontractor is the type of vehicle they are driving. You want the contractor with an old beat-up truck. You know the one: He has to park on the street because you don't want oil on the driveway. He's the guy with a pair of jumper cables as a permanent fixture in the vehicle. He's a handyman.

I do not use licensed contractors for all of my repairs. I use a licensed contractor when the job calls for it. The rest of the time I use a handyman.

For example, if I need to have a toilet replaced, I am not going to bring in a licensed plumbing contractor for that. Even I can replace a toilet. Yes, I know how to replace a toilet. And yes, you should turn the water off and drain the tank first. But just because I know how doesn't mean it's something I should be doing.

PITFALL: STAY OUT OF THE WAY

Don't let your enthusiasm run wild here and get in the way of making money. My first few rehabs I was there every day working side by side with my contractors. I called it working. The contractors called it helping. My wife called it stupid. She finally got it through my head that I was in the way. Your job as a Dumb Enough investor is to become a professional check writer. Spend your time doing the one thing no one in your company but you should be doing but you: making offers on property to buy.

Types of Contractors

When you have finally purchased your first property to rehab, what do you do first? The first day on all of my rehabs is a beehive of activity. I want all of my contractors there the first day. This would include:

- HVAC (heating and air conditioning) team

- Plumbers

- Painters

- Electricians

- Landscapers

Please see Chapter 21 for tips on how to assemble a dream team of contractors for rehabilitation. When you have your team assembled, you are ready to go to the next step.

PITFALL: MAKING IT TOO NICE

Please do not overspend on the rehab. By overspending I am referring to the need many rehabbers seem to have to make the home *too* nice. Yes, I am taking this home from being one of the worst in the neighborhood to being one of the nicest. And it is the little things, the attention to detail that helps us to transform the trash to cash. But don't get carried away.

Beautifying Without Overdoing It

These are the kinds of things you should do to improve the home. Start with the interior since this will require the bulk of your effort. The first thing you want to do is start with the ceilings. Ceilings add a great deal of light and brightness to a room. You want your ceilings to be clean and without any signs of past damage such as water spots. If you need to have the ceilings retextured, it can be done inexpensively. For a basic three-bedroom, two-bathroom, two-car-garage home with approximately 1,500 to 1,700 square feet, a good handyman should be able to resurface the ceilings in one to two days.

What do I mean by resurface? In most areas of the country, ceilings have for many years been finished with an acoustical spray

---

REPAIR TIPS

- ◆ Use a handyman (for most jobs)
- ◆ Use a Licensed Contractor (only when needed)
- ◆ HVAC -Heating and Air Conditioning (inspecting is a good idea)
- ◆ Electrical work (make sure the electrical panel is up to code)
- ◆ Plumbing (make sure there are no major problems)
- ◆ Landscaping (use day laborers instead of contractors)

BEAUTIFYING TIPS

- ◆ Resurfacing ceilings (e.g., when there's water damage)
- ◆ New light fixtures (e.g., ceiling fans for bedrooms, clear globe for other rooms)
- ◆ Improving walls (e.g., crown molding)
- ◆ Fixing/replacing doors (replace only when damaged)
- ◆ Flooring (e.g., carpet, vinyl for kitchen and bath)

sometimes called popcorn spray. It is a mushy liquid that is sprayed on the ceiling with the use of a spray rig. The spray rig has a wand that shoots this thick liquid on the ceiling. When it's dry, it looks as if someone put popcorn on the ceiling.

Popcorn spray needs a couple of days to dry before the ceilings are ready to paint. If you have a good handyman, he can rent a spray rig and paint the ceilings instead of you having to hire painters. After the ceilings have been finished, you should replace the light fixtures.

New light fixtures can be easily bought for less than twenty-five dollars apiece. What I use are the semicircular globes that fit flush against a base plate and can be purchased in either a clear globe or a frosted globe. Personally, I use the clear globe because it provides more light in the room. Remember: What we are going for here is clean and bright. This style of lighting fixture comes in three different sizes: 9-inch, 13-inch and 17-inch. The smaller sizes can be purchased for as little as $9.95. These fixtures are used in rooms other than the bedrooms and in bedrooms where the ceilings are too low for a ceiling fan to fit comfortably.

In almost all cases I put ceiling fans in the bedrooms. You can purchase nice fans in a brass finish with a fifty-two-inch blade for under fifty dollars. These fans come with blades that are reversible. One side of the blade is white while the other side is finished in a wood grain. Some of the fan blades have a light honey-color finish and some have a darker oak color to go along with the white side. I prefer the lighter honey finish because it brightens the room.

The next step is to add some charm to the walls. As you look from the ceilings to the walls, the first thing you should see is the crown molding. If the home doesn't have crown molding then you should add it. Crown molding is one of the inexpensive things you can do to a home to make it look terrific. It is sold in linear feet, which simply means it is sold in length or by the foot.

If your handyman doesn't know how to use a miter box, don't worry. He can use corner blocks. Let me point out that the proper use of a miter box is an absolute art form. To properly use a miter box, you have to be a craftsman in my book. To keep costs down, you shouldn't splurge on a craftsman. The handyman can finish the job with corner blocks.

Corner blocks allow you to do two things. First, you add a very nice-looking feature to your room. Second, you are able to speed up the refinishing process while eliminating the need for a miter-box craftsman. Corner blocks were built to eliminate the need for the tricky angle cuts required to make a piece of molding fit around a corner by creating a flat edge to butt the crown molding against. In other words, all of your molding saw cuts will be straight and flat. Even I can do that.

Now you are ready for walls. After any holes in the sheetrock have been repaired and the walls have been prepped for painting, you should replace all of the light switches and wall plugs. Please note I said *replace* the switches and plugs, not simply put new covers on them. A ten-count box of light switches is approximately $3.95. It will take your handyman around three to six minutes to replace a light switch, depending on how fast he is. This is an important investment. Remember to *turn the power off* when making these kinds of repairs.

PITFALL: TURN OFF THE POWER

Handymen know enough to get themselves and you into trouble sometimes. One of these trouble areas is electricity. Whenever your handymen are working on anything electrical, require them to turn the power off. I once saw a handyman knocked off a ladder and land several feet away because he was either too lazy or too overconfident in his abilities to turn off the power. It's not a pretty sight. Don't let this happen to you. The last thing anyone needs is an injured handyman with a starving attorney looking for someone to sue.

The next step is to check the baseboards. Almost any house I have ever worked on, or seen for that matter, has baseboards. Baseboards are the *boards* running around the room at the *base* of the walls, thus the term baseboards. These boards separate the walls from the floor and add a nice decorative touch. If your house doesn't have baseboards, add them.

Next on our journey from trash to cash are the doors. I try *not* to replace doors whenever possible. If a door has damage, then it should be replaced, but if it is just old and in need of some TLC, keep it. There are several items we can replace very cheaply to really dress up an old door. The most prominent item is the doorknob. I use good-looking, inexpensive brass knobs. Remember: Any time I speak of an item being finished in brass, I am talking about a shiny brass finish and not what is referred to as an antique or muted brass finish. There are three types of basic doorknob used in my trash-to-cash home.

First there is the key combo. These are knobs that require a key to unlock from the outside. These should be used for the front door, back door, and garage door. These locks have both a doorknob and deadbolt, and sell for less than thirty dollars per set. If you look on the front of the package, you will see the term "key code" followed by several numbers. These numbers allow us to purchase more than one set of key combo locks that all use the same keys.

Another doorknob you will be buying several of is the hall and closet knob. These are knobs used in areas where a lock is not required, such as a hall or closet, just as the name implies.

The last type of knob you will need is the bed and bath knob. Again, as the name implies, these are used for bedrooms ands bathrooms because they lock, usually with a push-button lock.

Between putting on a new knob and adding a fresh coat of paint, your doors will look great. The final finishing touch is replacing the hinges on the door. This is a small detail item that will add a lot to the appearance of your doors. Again I suggest buying the polished brass-finish hinges that sell for less than a dollar apiece. For two to three dollars, depending on whether the door is a three-hinge or a double-hinge door, you can spruce up the appearance of a door quickly and easily with new hinges.

The last item on your door makeover is the doorstop. You can purchase solid metal doorstops with a polished brass finish for about a dollar per pair. They have a white rubber tip on the end and add just one more small touch to the room.

Now for wall and carpet colors. At paint stores and home improvement stores all across the country, people order special custom colors of paint. If the mixed color doesn't match perfectly, the customer returns it to the store. The store employee writes "OOPS" across the top of the can; it is now sold for a few dollars per gallon even though it may have been twenty-five dollars per gallon originally. The first thing you should do is to purchase all of the OOPS in the white or tan color family. I do not care if it has a semi-gloss, satin, or flat finish as long as it is all latex paint.

Next comes the highly scientific part: You must buy a thirty-five-gallon trash can. Take all of the paint and pour it into the new trash can. Retrieve your modular mixing apparatus, otherwise known as a broom handle, and stir the paint together. It will all turn into a light tan color. Simply pour your new tan color back into the paint cans, and you have plenty of paint to completely finish this house. For your next house, simply add more paint to the mix, stir, and once again it is all the same color.

For carpeting I suggest using a light tan color also. I do not buy the lowest grade carpet, which is normally the base FHA carpet. I buy the next quality level up so that it doesn't look too cheap. I always replace the pad so that it looks brand new. Your flooring contractor can explain the difference in carpet grades better than I can.

How do you estimate the cost of replacing the flooring (carpet and vinyl) when you are looking at a property to buy, without having a carpet contractor come out to do an estimate? I created my own formula after I had completed three or four houses. The formula is very simple. Keep all of your flooring-related receipts—carpet, pad, installation, removal of the old carpet, taxes, replacement vinyl for the kitchen and baths. Take each house separately, and divide the total cost by the total square footage for the house. If it cost you $1,900 to replace all of the flooring in a 1,300-square-foot house, then your cost per square foot is $1.46. This number will help you greatly as you are looking at additional property to buy. Now you have a factor ($1.46) you can keep in your head to quickly compute a ballpark number it will cost you to replace the flooring when you are looking at additional property. Until you've completed a few houses, you'll have to use estimates and not paid estimates in your formula.

Here are some other things you might consider doing to make a good impression on home buyers:

- ◆ Clear plants and foliage away from windows so that more light comes in. A bright home will appear cheery and welcoming.

- ◆ Make sure the entryway makes a good impression. This includes replacing the house numbers, fixing the doorbell, making the door look as new as possible, and putting out a doormat. The entryway is one of the first things a buyer sees, so make sure it looks new and clean.

- Clean the entire house and remove as much clutter as possible. Leaving the rooms empty makes them look bigger and allows the prospective buyer to imagine themselves into the space.

- Get rid of any foul odors. In fact, you may want to add some pleasant smells to make it seem more homey. Cinnamon potpourri in the kitchen, for example, can help remind the buyer of freshly baked goods. Fresh paint will help make sure the place smells new, but make sure there are no overwhelming construction odors like carpet glue.

- Install shelving in the closets.

Chapter Summary

When beginning rehabilitation on your HUD or foreclosed home, first determine what repairs need to be done and figure out your budget. Then put together a team that will quickly do all the repairs necessary to make your house saleable. Don't fall into the trap of trying to do everything yourself. Make the investment—it will pay off in the long term. But don't go too far either. You want to make the house saleable without overpaying for repairs.

In the next chapter we are going to redo the kitchen and bathrooms. These are so important they warrant their own chapter.

Pitfalls Recap

THE GENERAL CONTRACTOR/HANDYMAN TRAP. Remember the person we are looking for is the handyman. If the contractor is driving the new, extended cab, long bed, dual rear-wheeled Silverado pickup, that's not our guy. We want the handyman with the truck voted most likely to be mistaken for Sanford and Son. Make sure it's you and not the contractor making the huge profits on this deal.

STAY OUT OF THE WAY! Our job is to become a professional check writer, not to be able to build a house from the ground up using only a Swiss Army pocket knife. Let the contractors do their job and you do yours. Yours is to make more offers. Period.

MAKING IT TOO NICE. Remember, *you are not going to live there.*

TURN OFF THE POWER! There are enough surprises in rehabbing a house, there's no need to make it a shocking experience as well.

REHABILITATING HOUSES

TURNING TRASH INTO CASH

"YOU GOTTA have heart" says a song from the early seventies. In our business, the heart of any home is the kitchen. Male readers must understand it's the women who make the buying decisions when it comes to a home purchase. Sure, lots of homes are sold to single men, but the vast majority of home-buying decisions in America are made by women. Understanding this is a great help to us when we are rehabilitating a house.

The benefit to us comes from knowing the "heart of the matter" and how to best please our typical customer, the female homebuyer. If the kitchen in any home is the heart, then the bathrooms are the soul of the property. This chapter is devoted to the rehabilitation process for the heart and soul of home, the kitchen and bathrooms.

The Kitchen

Let's take a look at the kitchen first. The kitchen is the heart of a home because it is where we congregate. It's where the food is kept, so we naturally gravitate to the kitchen.

While redoing a kitchen, we want to make sure to remember the number-one rule of rehabilitation: Make it bright and clean.

PITFALL: BRIGHT AND CLEAN

It is very easy to get carried away with "bright and clean." You might, for example, decide the best color to paint kitchens is a nice bright white because it would create the brightest and cleanest kitchen. Yes, it would, but remember when you rehabilitate that you are walking a delicate line between "bright and clean" and "cold and austere." An operating room is "bright and clean," but I wouldn't necessarily want to sit down to a home-cooked meal in one.

Our objective is to keep it as bright and clean as possible, yet also keep it as warm as possible.

In the kitchen, lighting is more important than in any other room in the house. You should look for a fixture that sheds a lot of light. The domed fixtures mentioned in the last chapter work well for a kitchen as well. Using these fixtures throughout the home creates a good unified design. Choose the largest light you can without making it look out of place. I prefer a domed fixture with a 17-inch base for the kitchen.

Remember to use clear, not frosted, glass for fixtures. Though frosted glass puts out a softer, more diffused light, it's more important to have lots of light, so choose clear over frosted.

You will also want to use the greatest watt light bulbs you can safely use in the fixture, adding a bulb in *all* of the receptacles. Please don't be cheap when it comes to light bulbs; buy a dozen or so and keep them in the kitchen cabinets for replacements. You may be able to buy in bulk.

Personally, I put new light bulbs in all of the fixtures throughout the house. It lessens the likelihood of there being a burned-out bulb in a fixture when the buyer looks at the home. Since you can't know which of the people looking at the house will become the buyer, it's better to be safe than sorry.

As far as the ceilings are concerned, I suggest the same popcorn acoustic used in the rest of the house. The ceilings should definitely be white.

Should crown moldings be used in a kitchen? The answer is a resounding "yes." This is one of those areas where going the extra mile will pay off with handsome dividends.

Go out in your market area at least once a month and visit new subdivisions. Organize your day so that you can look at several new homes in a single afternoon. You will get some great decorating ideas while doing this. The idea of using crown molding in the kitchen came to me while visiting homes in my area. I noticed that the more expensive homes I looked at had crown molding in the kitchen while the cheaper homes took the shortcut of not putting in the molding. I figured out that it costs less than $200 to add molding for most kitchens in our bread-and-butter market.

Bread-and-butter houses are three bedrooms, two baths, with a two-car garage. Most were built in the mid-sixties to early seventies and range in size anywhere from 1,200 to 1,700 square feet.

In most cases you will *not* have to replace the cabinets in these homes. Do not get carried away and spend too much money on the rehabilitation. You are not going to be living there. Homes older than our bread-and-butter homes may have to have new cabinets installed. If this is the case, make sure you compare the "per linear foot" costs of cabinets to get the best buy. I have found the best buys to be at home improvement stores. You do not have to buy the cheapest cabinets offered, but don't get carried away either.

Call several cabinetmakers as well to make sure you're getting reasonable prices. Ask questions like, "Could you achieve the same results by replacing the doors and not the entire cabinet?" If you take a look at the cabinets, you'll see that most of the visible area is simply the cabinet doors. Adding new doors will make it look as if the house has entirely new cabinets. You may also be able to have the exterior of the cabinets refinished and not have to replace them. A good cabinetmaker or a good painter will be able to do wonders with refinishing. Weigh your options, and go for the one that provides the best look for the least amount of money.

Countertops are another area where you can quickly overspend if you are not careful. If the countertops are ugly, and I mean *ugly*, don't have a knee-jerk reaction and assume they must be replaced. The worst ones I have seen are a lovely avocado green color. If the countertops are in good condition, you can have them resurfaced.

This is a trick of the trade I learned from a friend who manages commercial property. I had called her one day to ask her advice on replacing countertops. She referred me to a contractor who refinished countertops. Once I got him on the phone, I realized how much money he could save me. The contractor simply sprays an epoxy-based paint over the existing finish. This special epoxy paint looks great when it has dried and provides a scratch-resistant surface to the countertop. Epoxy paint comes in almost any color, and you can have a smooth or rough texture to the finish. It even comes with decorative small specks of an accent color mixed in if you really want to get carried away.

The sink is an area where you can score lots of brownie points with your prospective buyer. Most of the homes in your target price range will have stainless steel sinks with a vegetable sprayer. There is only one bad thing about these vegetable sprayers: *They don't work.* Usually the sprayer only lets out a small dribble of water. Prospective buyers will likely make their way into the kitchen at some point during the showing and pull the sprayer out for a quick test. How embarrassing would it be to lose a sale and a profit of twenty thousand dollars because the vegetable sprayer doesn't work?

There is a remedy. You can now buy the faucet with the sprayer built into the faucet. They always work and there is usually more pressure from the faucet sprayer than there is from the old type. Moet and Delta make a very nice unit which sells for around $150. This unit comes in three basic finishes, tan, white, and chrome.

When you have the unit installed, you will discover there are four holes in most older sinks. These holes were filled by the hot water line, cold water line, and the faucet. To the far right of those three holes is the fourth hole, which was used for the vegetable sprayer. When you replace the old faucet assembly with your new Moen or Delta faucet/sprayer combination unit, you will have an empty hole where the old vegetable sprayer was. For approximately seventeen dollars you can buy a soap dispenser that fits perfectly into the fourth hole. The soap dispenser also comes in the same three finishes as the faucet: tan, white, and chrome.

If your sink is stainless steel and looks too old or looks as if it was not really stainless, you may want to replace it. This can appear to be an expensive process, but a steel sink finished in white is cheaper than most stainless steel sinks. Now you have a new sink with a new faucet/sprayer combo, and a new soap dispenser. In addition, the kitchen has resurfaced countertops and cabinets with new doors.

Looking at the kitchen from the top down, our ceilings have been resurfaced and repainted. The light fixture has been replaced, and we have crown molding all around the room. The cabinets look new, and the countertops and sink either are new or look new. Our kitchen is shaping up nicely.

Of course the walls receive the same treatment as the rest of the house. The type of treatment used will vary in different parts of the country.

Looking at new subdivisions is another great way to determine what is the most popular and accepted style in your area.

Now you need to address the flooring. Floors in the kitchen are normally covered in vinyl. This makes for good wear and easy care in a room where messes are the order of the day. Pick a good vinyl for these bread-and-butter houses. The pattern and the color should of course blend easily with the décor in the rest of the house.

When you are redoing the kitchen, you should take a hard look at the appliances. In almost all cases I replace them. You will want to buy basic models for this. A new basic stove or range has more appeal to the average buyer than a more expensive used unit. It is part of our makeup as Americans; we prefer new. Look in the yellow pages for an appliance outlet where they sell "scratch and dent units." If the damage to a stove or a dishwasher is on the sides or the back of the unit, it will not be visible once it is installed. The appliance company cannot sell these units for the same price as a new, undamaged unit. You can replace the dishwasher and the range for around $500 to $600.

The garbage disposal is very inexpensive to replace. If the unit currently in the house works but is loud, replace it. Old units in perfect working order will usually make a lot of noise. They sound like you've just started the engines on an old DC3 airplane. You want a quiet garbage disposal. This new quiet unit can be purchased for under fifty dollars.

A very nice touch to give the house much more of a homey feel is to put a couple of hand towels and some potpourri on the counter.

Bathrooms

Now you need to examine the bathrooms. Bathrooms are the second most important feature your house has to offer. Like the kitchen, the bathroom needs to be bright and clean.

Let's start at the top. The ceilings should be retextured or repainted as they have been in the rest of the house. Yes, we will be putting crown molding in the bathroom. This really adds an expensive feel to the low-end starter homes.

If your bathroom has an exhaust fan with a plastic light cover, be sure to examine the plastic cover to see if it has turned yellow. Old plastic will turn yellow or brown and become very brittle. If this has happened, replace it. A new exhaust fan is well under $30 and should be quieter and more attractive.

The light fixture in many cases is above the mirror over the sink. I prefer the bar lights fixture. Bar lights have a base plate, which is a rectangular bar with three or more light bulbs screwed directly into the bar. If you use a bar light, it is important to choose the right type of light bulb. Many companies produce a designer bulb. A designer bulb is simply a ball-shaped bulb produced in clear or frosted glass. In most cases I will go for the clear bulb as it gives the most light.

If you use a countertop refinisher in the kitchen, be sure to have him look at the bathrooms as well. It is not unusual to have a bathroom where the tile is in great shape, but the color or pattern is so bad it haunts you in your dreams at night. The countertop refinisher can also refinish the tile in the bathroom. This is a much cheaper process than having it replaced.

Should the toilet need replacing, you can easily purchase a new one with all of the guts already in the tank for less than $75. Don't forget to turn the water off first and drain the tank. Also make sure the handyman puts a rag in the sewer pipe hole while he's working on this or the smell will kill you. Remember he has to take the rag *out* before putting the new toilet in place. Having to go back and remove it later is not a pretty sight. Think about it and you'll get the picture. Do not even think about reading the next paragraph without rereading this paragraph again. You can thank me later.

The bathroom sink in many bread-and-butter homes is a single cabinet with the sink sitting on top of the cabinet. These units are cheaply replaced for under $125. With new vinyl on the floor, your bathroom is complete. A couple of well-placed hand towels, a roll of toilet paper, and a soap dispenser and you're ready to go.

Chapter Summary

The kitchen and bathrooms of a house can really close a sale. Pay special attention when you rehabilitate these areas of the house, because they are the heart of the home. When prospective buyers see newly renovated kitchens and bathrooms they are more likely to buy the house.

Pitfalls Recap

BRIGHT AND CLEAN. Remember we are walking a delicate line here between "bright and clean" and "cold and austere."

FORECLOSURE OR
PRE-FORECLOSURE?
THAT IS THE QUESTION

THE FORECLOSURE rate is the highest it has ever been in the United States, and it is going up. Foreclosure is a natural by-product of home ownership, and U.S. home ownership is at an all-time high. Real estate investors are entering a time of unprecedented opportunity in the foreclosure arena.

How does a foreclosure happen? The first event that triggers the foreclosure process is when the homeowner is unable to send checks to the mortgage company or bank. After a few months of nonpayment and several letters from the mortgage company, someone at the mortgage company makes the decision to turn the homeowner's file over to an attorney to start the foreclosure process.

PITFALL: BUT HOW DOES IT WORK HERE?

In classes all over the country students ask me the very same question. It would be easy for me to spend the next fifty plus pages telling you about the differences in the foreclosure process from state to state, such as whether your state is a judicial or nonjudicial foreclosure state or whether your state has a redemption period. But there is the possibility of giving you too much information for your own good. I want to keep you moving forward to start your real estate investing career, so I am giving you a homework assignment.

I'm dead serious. I am giving you an assignment right now. For those of you who are serious about the business, this will be very helpful. I want you to call a title company, escrow company, or real estate attorney and ask them to walk you through the steps necessary to foreclose on a homeowner. This exercise is going to serve you in several ways:

1. You will receive a Cliff Notes version of the foreclosure process for your state.

2. If you are paying attention, you will start establishing a relationship with the person you called, and this is a good bonus. Title companies, escrow companies, and real estate attorneys are all good sources for deals. They may not be able to keep your pipeline full but they can certainly add a few deals a year to it.

Please note today's date. If you are calling a title company and if today's date is in the last week of the month,

> you should wait. Title companies are very busy the last
> week of the month. Be respectful of their time and you
> may form a very profitable relationship.

OK, you've completed your homework assignment, and we can move forward. You now have a basic idea of how the process works in your state. Let's spend the next few pages on how to find foreclosures and then walk through the few steps it takes to get you in the game.

Whenever you are dealing with the foreclosure market, you will need to have some cash. Cash is required from almost all institutions that have taken over property via the foreclosure process. This could be a good time for you to reread Chapter 5.

The two primary sources for foreclosed property are banks and mortgage companies. Several years ago the law changed, and banks are now allowed to make a profit on property they have foreclosed on. This major change has had a great impact on how we as real estate investors work with these institutions. Most banks and mortgage companies with foreclosed property now contract the services of a Realtor, real estate agent, or broker to assist in the liquidation of these properties.

PITFALL: OUR MARKET IS RED HOT SO THERE CAN'T BE ANY FORECLOSURES

This comment is made over and over to me as I criss-cross the country teaching about real estate. Do not be lulled into the false notion that, just because you live in an area where the real estate market is red hot, there are no foreclosures. Quite the opposite is true. The southern California market is one of the hottest markets in the country. The southern California market, specifically Los Angeles, is also the nation's foreclosure capital. The five counties making up the Greater Los

Angeles area have substantially more foreclosures than any other area in the country.

How can this be? Let's have a quick overview of the marketplace and answer a few basic questions before we move on to the steps to put you into the foreclosure business. Let me ask you this: Do people get divorced where you live? Do people get laid off, get sick, get transferred or even die where you live? OK, now you know how foreclosures happen even in a hot market. Maybe you're thinking, "Why don't these people living in hot real estate markets just sell their home at a discount, pay off their mortgage, and move on instead of going through foreclosure?" Great question. I can't tell you why people allow themselves to be foreclosed on even when they have a big chunk of equity in their property, but they do. It is a fact of life, and it's one that isn't about to change just because you decided to get in the business.

If almost all the banks and mortgage companies are using Realtors, real estate agents, and brokers to market their REO (Real Estate Owned) property, how do we find them? It's simple. We call the banks and ask for their names and numbers. It's simple and extremely frustrating. Why, you ask? Because most banks are not used to this kind of request. You will certainly have to go to the branch manager, and you'll probably also have to go to the regional manager to find someone who can tell you the names and phone numbers of the agents the bank works with. An employee of one of the largest banks in America told me point-blank that they did not have any foreclosures and seemed insulted that I thought they did. Do not be surprised to find this level of ignorance when you start your quest. It is definitely worth your time to push the matter. One Realtor, real estate agent, or broker who represents the foreclosed property of a bank or mortgage company can really make a difference.

PITFALL: THE INABILITY TO CLOSE

Developing a relationship with the real estate professionals who represent the banks and mortgage companies can provide you with a steady stream of deals. There is a major pitfall you must be aware of. Don't ever submit a contract on one of these deals if you aren't sure you will be able to close. Not closing with a foreclosure agent will likely cost you the relationship, and the relationship could be worth several million dollars over the life of your investing career. There is too much at stake for you not to treat this relationship with the kid gloves it deserves.

An additional source of foreclosed property is what we commonly refer to as "finance companies." These companies normally specialize in second mortgages with high interest rates. They will take on larger risk than most banks or mortgage companies. They are willing to take these risks because they charge higher interest rates for the loans. Because finance companies take on high-risk loans, they tend to get a fair number of these properties back through the foreclosure process. Once again, most of these companies are represented by Realtors, real estate agents, or brokers. A short phone call will likely produce the needed contact information and may even get the current list of properties faxed to you.

Offer a Shorter Closing Date

One way to distinguish yourself from everyone else who is bidding on these REO properties is to offer a shorter than normal closing date. The normal and customary closing time in the United States is thirty days. I know it runs forty-five days for HUD properties, but if you are dealing with a Realtor, real estate agent, or broker who represents a lending institution, this will do wonders for you. When you ask for a shorter than normal closing time, you automatically build your credibility with the institution. Institutions work on different time frames than you and I do, and they do things for very different reasons. You may not even be the highest bid, but you could still get the property simply because of the closing date.

You might wonder why institutions, especially banks, that have so much money would take a deep discount (which they regularly do) on a piece of property. It's an excellent question, one I've heard many times through the years. I asked several professional acquaintances and found one of them was willing to let me in on how the institutions think. If we think as they do for a minute, we can easily understand why they do this.

Let's follow a $100,000 CD purchased at the bank. These funds now add to the bank's deposit base and add to their lending reserves. The lending reserve is what is used by the banking regulators to determine how much money the bank can lend. My friend tells me the banks are able to lend $800,000 against the $100,000 CD. Now, I understand this must fall into the category of new math, but the more I learned about the banking system, the more it appeared to me that one check bounced by a college student recovering from a drunken fraternity party at a junior college somewhere in the Midwest could cause the entire banking system to collapse. I have been assured, however, this is not the case.

This 8 to 1 lending ratio also works in reverse, which means if the banks were to make eight $100,000 loans against our original $100,000 CD, and if one of these loans were to go bad and become a nonperforming asset, it would tie up $800,000 of the bank's lending ability. So how do banks make their money? Most of us believe it is from the high fees they nickel-and-dime us to death with at every turn, but it's not true. They make money from the interest on loans they make. So if they suddenly cannot loan $800,000 because of this one bad loan they made, it makes sense for them to take a loss on it and get it out of their portfolio. That's why they will take what appears to be a huge discount on a foreclosed property. It is also why offering them a shorter closing date will make you more attractive. The sooner they get this loan out of their portfolio the better.

Five Steps to Buying a Foreclosed Home

Here are five simple steps to get you into the middle of foreclosed property in your area.

FORECLOSURE STEP 1: *Contacts.* Take a few hours in the next three days and call at least five different banking institutions or finance companies in your area to find out who represents their foreclosed/REO property. Once you have a contact name and phone number, call and introduce yourself. Make sure you ask to be put on their fax distribution list. If they have a property you can close on within two weeks, tell the representative.

Once you have completed these calls, go to your yellow pages and look up auction companies. Call every auction company listed in the yellow pages and ask them if they auction real estate. Most, but not all, do. Ask the ones that do to add you to their mailing list for future auctions.

The last part of Step 1 is to complete a Google search on the Internet for "foreclosures." You will be stunned when you get over a half million sites specializing in foreclosure information. If you do a second search with your state placed after the word "foreclosures," it will reduce the number significantly. In my second search it

---

THE SIMPLE 5-STEP PROCESS FOR FORECLOSURES

Foreclosure Step #1 Contacts

Foreclosure Step #2 Market Value

Foreclosure Step #3 Having the Cash Ready for a Quick Close

Foreclosure Step #4 Making the Offer

Foreclosure Step #5 Create Deposits

---

dropped the number of sites to around a hundred and fifty thousand. With these few steps you should start to see several deals per month that are very attractive.

FORECLOSURE STEP 2: *Market value.* Every process for evaluation I use starts with the "traditional" market value of the house. The only way we can establish the traditional market value of a property is by using comparable sales (comps). Without the traditional market value of the property, you have no idea if the price you are bidding is a value or not. Get your comps from Realtors, real estate agents, and brokers. Or you can do as I earlier suggested and become an associate member of the local board of Realtors.

FORECLOSURE STEP 3: *Having the cash ready for a quick close.* We know we are going to have cash involved if we are dealing with an institution on a foreclosed property. It would be wise to start lining up your funds immediately. Remember to use the script I gave you in Chapter 5, and don't give the farm away.

FORECLOSURE STEP 4: *Making the offer.* When you are dealing with the representative of a foreclosed property, the only offer they are interested in is a contractual offer. You will have to use the state-approved "Purchase and Sales" contract. Go back to the "Blood, Sweat, and Tears" formula found in Chapter 6, and make sure your offer is favorable for you. Remember: All offers represented by Realtors, real estate agents, or brokers must be in contractual form or they don't exist.

FORECLOSURE STEP 5: *Create deposits.* This is a friendlier way to say, sell the property. I think of marketing this way, as creating deposits.

Chapter Summary

Foreclosed homes can be incredibly profitable. It pays to find out about the foreclosure process in your state. Then make contacts with a number of people who represent these properties. Follow the five steps to buying foreclosures and you will be well on your way to riches.

Does this seem simple to you? It is. Remember: This is a simple business; it is not an easy business. With a little grit and determination, this business is like the genie in the bottle—it will grant your wishes.

In the next chapter we're going to learn about a part of the business where there is even more opportunity than in foreclosures.

Pitfalls Recap

BUT HOW DOES IT WORK HERE? Do your homework assignment and find out. Don't be lazy, there is too much money in our business for you not to get involved.

OUR MARKET IS RED HOT SO THERE CAN'T BE ANY FORECLOSURES. Do not be lulled into the false notion that just because you live in an area where the real estate market is red hot there are no foreclosures. Quite the opposite is true.

THE INABILITY TO CLOSE. Don't ever submit a contract on one of these deals if you aren't sure you will be able to close.

PRE-FORECLOSURE

THE PREFERRED CHOICE

PRE-FORECLOSURE, as Ernie Kessler says, "conjures up the cartoon image of a woman being tied to the railroad tracks by the evil banker and then the hero comes riding in on the white horse to save the day."

Aren't we as real estate investors the heroes riding in on the white horse? Yes, we are. It is our duty to let everyone in our marketplace know the truth about foreclosure before they go through with it.

Foreclosure Is a (Financial) Fate Worse Than (Financial) Death

After having conversations with mortgage brokers from all over the country, it is an overwhelming conclusion that foreclosure is worse than bankruptcy when it comes to your credit report and your future prospects of buying a home. Knowing this, isn't it our duty to let everyone in pre-foreclosure know the truth about what they are about to do? You bet it is. This little bit of education will help you be of more service to your community and buy more property in pre-foreclosure.

Just in case anyone is wondering, pre-foreclosure is simply the status of a property in the foreclosure process that hasn't been sold on the courthouse steps yet. While a property is in the pre-foreclosure stage, the homeowner is still in control. Dealing with the homeowner can be a lot easier for us and certainly presents more options than dealing directly with the lending institution.

Step 1: Locate a Foreclosure Listing Services

To get this pre-foreclosure machine rolling you first have to learn where to find pre-foreclosures. In every city in America it is the law that a foreclosure must be publicly posted for a specific number of days, which varies by state, before a property can be foreclosed on and then sold on the courthouse steps. The most readily accepted form of "public posting" in our country is the newspaper. So the first place you can look for pre-foreclosures in is the newspaper. Although this is a very inexpensive way to find the information we need, it is also the least user-friendly.

In almost every one of our nation's approximately 3,200 counties there is a legal or "business journal" that captures this information for publication to the attorneys in the county. There will be more covered in this publication than just pre-foreclosures. This business journal will also list all of the bankruptcy filings, divorces, probates, and any other procedure requiring public notice. Many of these business journals will make their publication available electronically. This is how you will want to buy this information.

These pre-foreclosure lists should cost you less than $100 per month. This expenditure will be some of the best money you will ever spend. In the last chapter you were given an assignment. You did do your homework didn't you? Some things never change. Before you leave this chapter, go back and complete your homework assignment. Got it done? Good, because the Internet search you did probably provides you with a ton of listing services specializing in pre-foreclosure lists. One of these companies will be perfect for you, but it is going to require a little effort on your part to wade through the thousands of Web sites to find the right one.

PITFALL: YOU'D BE LOCO NOT TO GO LOCAL

This is my opinion only, but I believe you will be better served by using a local service than by being sucked into the marketing machine of some of the national services. One of these national services I checked out is so pesky with their barrage of marketing e-mails they make all of those high-pressure timeshare sales people look like rank amateurs. See if you can locate a local service. You should be looking for a service that provides you with timely information, including the homeowner's name and address, a brief description of the property, the lender's name, the name of the trustee attorney, and information on approximately how far behind the homeowner is, what type of loan it is, and when the loan was originated.

Step 2: Arrange for Enough Cash to Cover the Deal

Know before you ever start your pre-foreclosure marketing machine that you will have to have some cash. There is only one way you will regularly stop a foreclosure, and that is with cash. Cold, hard cash.

Lending institutions could care less about how creative we are when it comes to pre-foreclosure, the only thing they want to see from us is the dough. You now know how to raise private investor money, so private investors should be fertile ground for your business. If you need a refresher on this part of the process, see Chapter 5.

Step 3: Write and Mail the Pre-Foreclosure Letter.

Many gurus of the foreclosure/pre-foreclosure side of our business will tell you to go out unannounced and knock on the doors of the people whose homes are in pre-foreclosure. They say this will get you a greater number of responses than using direct mail. I am absolutely sure you will get a great number of responses. I'm just not sure it's the kind of responses you will be looking for. I've gotten these types of sales orders before—you know, get out and stay out. This is why I don't advocate just stopping by. I don't want anyone I teach to become a crime statistic either. Many people in pre-foreclosure aren't in a good mood.

Personally I use direct mail. I have found it to be very successful in reaching this market. Figure 10-1 is a copy of the letter I send out every month. Many of you will want to use this letter, and that's OK with me with one very important stipulation: If you are going to use this letter, you must first write out the letter by hand and then type it into your computer yourself. In essence, I want you to write it out twice so that you know exactly what the letter says. This is very important because when people call you, they are responding to what you said in the letter. If you don't seem to know what they are talking about, it will be like throwing cold water in their face. Believe me, they will not want to do business with you if you are not sincere.

Step 4: Use the WOW Method to Weed Out the Bad Deals

Use the WOW method described in Chapter 4 to determine whether this is really a deal you want to go after.

Dear Homeowner,

I want to buy your house. No, I'm not a Realtor, and I don't work for a real estate company either. I'm not interested in just "listing" your home or even showing it.

I want to buy your house.

And if my information is correct, you may want to sell your house. If that's the case, read the important information below and give me a call right away. I may have the perfect solution for you.

There are many reasons why people may need to sell a house quickly. Relocation. Job loss. Divorce. When things like this happen, it's easy to fall behind on your payments. I know. I've been there.

If this sounds familiar, I can help—even if your home is already in the foreclosure process.

The most important thing is to not to give up.

You may be tempted to just let the bank foreclose, but that would be a terrible mistake. It will ruin your credit for a long, long time. Trust me: That's a situation you don't want to be in.

Selling a house is usually an expensive and complicated process. That's why real estate agents make thousands and thousands of dollars on a single sale.

But, if I buy your house, **I promise there will be no excessive fees or commissions to pay**.

And you certainly won't have to be subjected to total strangers stomping through your home and snooping around your closets and drawers. Perhaps the worst part of it is that these strangers all seem to silently judge you, your lifestyle, your current predicament, and every other aspect of your life. Most of them probably aren't even seriously considering buying your house. **You've been through enough of that, haven't you?**

Well, I'm associated with a group of private investors that buy from [X] to [X] houses per month—houses like yours! I buy houses in almost every area of [insert town] and every price range. I use private funds that require

FIGURE 10-1

no long, drawn-out bank approvals.

In fact, in the past few months, I've bought [X] houses in this area, so you know I'm serious. **I'm as serious about buying your house as you are about selling it.** And, as I mentioned, above, I'm not a real estate agent. There's a very big difference…

An agent lists houses and then hopes they sell. I **buy** houses!

If you're the one with the house for sale, you know **that's a huge difference.**

I may be able to buy your house in as little as 7 days, and save your good name and credit. I'm experienced at working with mortgage companies and can probably work out a deal in which everyone wins.

Of course, you have the option of selling it yourself. After all, who knows more about your house than you do? But think about this: How many houses have you bought and sold in your life? Two or three? You haven't had to solve even a fraction of the typical problems that always seem to come up right before closing the deal.

Do you really want to risk having a potential buyer slip away just because you're not used to dealing with the numerous details of a real estate transaction? This is where I come in. My business is solving problems…especially the kind you find when you're dealing with a complicated real estate deal.

What are your options?

You could significantly drop the price and hope someone will take your house for peanuts, but can you afford to do that? What if you don't have enough equity to discount your house?

You could try and turn the house over to the bank, but that won't work either. They'll just come after you for the money and ruin your credit anyway.

Every month it takes to sell your home adds to your enormous debt. But, it gets worse…if you leave, what's going to stop vandals from breaking in and spray-painting the walls or flooding the house? You're still responsible for the damage. The hole just gets deeper and deeper.

Here's a better solution!

If your property qualifies (I think it will), I guarantee to provide you with a written offer within 48 hours after I see it. Without using the real estate lingo, I'll explain everything to you in plain English and be direct and honest with you from start to finish.

If we come to an agreement, I can pay you *cash* with no contingencies and close in a few days if needed. I'll take care of the paperwork and make all the arrangements, and you can move on with your life!

I don't know your particular reasons for selling, but I do know how to get your house closed quickly and professionally. Because I work with private funds, I can usually do so in as little as 48 to 72 hours.

Don't you owe it to yourself to at least find out what I can do for you? All you have to do is call me direct. Please call (XXX) 555–1212.

Sincerely,

[Your Name]

[Your title]

P.S. If you want to sell your house in the quickest, easiest and least painful way possible, you simply must get in touch with me—*RIGHT NOW!* You have nothing to lose—**except that big mortgage payment.**

PITFALL: STAY AWAY FROM SKINNY DEALS

If you don't want to raise skinny kids, stay away from skinny deals. One of the leading reasons people fail in our business is that they jump all over a deal because it's available and not because it's a good deal. If you cannot clear approximately 20 percent of the total sales price as profit, the deal is probably just too skinny. You must have at least 20 percent because all of these deals will require some cash and almost all of them will require some repair work, even if it is only cosmetic.

Don't become a victim of "dealitis." Make sure you approach this business with the simple tools I am giving you.

Step 5: Make the Offer

So far you've located a pre-foreclosure listing service, you know you will have to have investor money lined up, and you have a sample direct mail letter. Next comes the offer. To figure out what to offer, take a look at Chapter 13. Use Figure 13-1 to figure out exactly what you can offer, and then use Figure 13-2 to create the offer letter.

Many of these people in pre-foreclosure will start calling you in response to your direct mail letter. You will discover they have some or no equity. Here is a very good way to deal with this: an excellent way to create a Win/Win transaction in the pre-foreclosure market is to allow the homeowner to keep a portion of their equity in the form of cash when you resell the property. As an example, if someone has $105,000 dollars worth of net equity in their home, you could offer them $20,000 now or $35,000 later—later being when you have resold the property. They will only get back a portion of their equity, but something is better than nothing.

Keep in mind, this is a portion of their equity, not their entire equity. "Net equity" is the term I use for "profit" in a pre-foreclosure deal. You have to take into consideration the amount of the back payments. Those back payments have to be made to stop the foreclosure process. After you have stopped the foreclosure, you will have to make the mortgage payments going forward so the property doesn't end up back in foreclosure. The attorney fees have to be paid. There are maintenance issues such as utilities, landscaping, the pool, and whatever repairs you have to make. All of this takes cash. When you figure out net equity, you have to subtract all these costs from what they have in equity. Before you make this kind of offer, make sure you have enough cash to cover it all.

PITFALL: NOT GETTING ENOUGH INVESTOR CASH TO COVER IT ALL

Remember that when you are agreeing on the amount of money your private investor is going to put up, you must make sure you take everything into consideration. By everything I mean catching up on the back payments, including the attorney fees, six months of future mortgage payments while you are marketing the property, six months of utilities and home maintenance, and six months of advertising costs. Your private investor should be covering all of these costs, and there should be no interest payments required until the house is resold. I know this is repetitive but you can't afford not to have this drilled into your head.

One of my favorite deal stories is about a house that resembled a small hotel. Several months ago, I had finished my normal pre-foreclosure monthly routine. I had purchased my pre-foreclosure list. I had mailed the approximately 1,400 letters to everyone on the list and started getting phone calls within three to four days of the mailing. One of the calls was from a very nice lady. As usual I started going through the WOW with her. I almost dropped the phone when she said her home had been recently appraised for $1.2 million. I know for many of you reading this book, depending on what part of the country you live in, $1.2 million isn't the be-all and end-all in home ownership, but in Fort Worth, Texas, $1.2 million is one whopper of a house. She told me there was an outstanding balance on the property of $675,000 and that she and her husband were six months behind in payments. Six back payments on a $1.2 million home will get your attention. They were $72,000 behind before adding the attorney's fees. I told her I would review the numbers and see if there was anything I could do. It was at this point that her husband entered the picture. Being the man of the house, he was now going to be in control. I called him back within forty-eight hours with the best offer I have ever made a home-owner. The offer was this: I'll bring you a cashier's check for $100,000, I'll catch up all of your back payments and attorney's fees, I'll make all of the payments going forward until the house is sold, and I'll keep the property properly maintained. Once I have sold the property, I'll get my $100,000 back and all the money I have invested in the process. Everything above that we will split fifty-fifty. There was a long pause on the other end of the phone, and then the man responded with, "I'm going to pass, because I think you're making too much money on the deal." A few minutes later my wife threw a bucket of cold water on me to revive me. If he had worked with me, the worst possible deal for the seller was $100,000. Since he didn't work with me, the worst possible scenario for him actually happened. The foreclosure date arrived, and the property was sold on the courthouse steps to the mortgage com-pany. Yes, that does mean the sellers got zip, zero, nada of their equity, and it happens all the time all over the country. Don't ask me why I didn't buy it for myself; my wife has already asked me a few hundred times.

PITFALL: THE LURE OF THE BIG-DOLLAR HOUSE

Please note, even though I believe the opportunity to purchase a huge, high-end house to live in is great and getting better, please do not start putting these homes into your investment portfolio. High-end homes will put you out of business in a hurry. I know too many

investors who have tried this route only to go broke. I
tried this route personally and it almost ran me out of
the business. Stay in the average- to lower-priced
homes and you'll be just fine.

If you are looking for a personal residence I believe now there are
unprecedented opportunities to purchase a foreclosure or pre-foreclosure. The business opportunities are tremendous, but if you're
looking for a home yourself, especially a high-end home, the market
may be the best it's ever been.

THE MOST IMPORTANT PART OF STEP 5. I want to shift gears
here and ask you to read these next few paragraphs twice before moving forward. In our business there are a few mistakes that can end up
costing you dearly. This one is one I want to highlight even more, so
rather than listing it as a Pitfall, I am making it a Super Pitfall.

SUPER PITFALL: WARNING. . . THIS IS A DEEP HOLE

Any time we are involved in a real estate transaction
requiring us to take cash out of our pocket or bank
account, we are never going to do it unless we have a
contract (purchase and sales agreement) and the deed
to the property. I'll get more into getting the deed in
the next chapter. In real estate, there is no such thing
as a verbal contract. A verbal contract isn't worth the
paper it isn't written on.

In the pre-foreclosure market its called "cash for keys." Cash for
keys is another way of saying that we are never going to take the word
of a seller of a pre-foreclosure about moving out of the property until

they drop the keys to the now-vacant house into our hot little hands. If you violate this rule, you will be telling a story worthy of publication. Would you like to see my scars?

One of my favorite deals took a while to become one of my favorites. It started out as a royal pain in the tush and an embarrassment that I could be so gullible. A pre-foreclosure came my way from my direct mail letter. The seller was a single mom with two small children who had recently gone through a divorce. The husband had given her the house out of spite. He knew there was no way for her to keep this high-end house with over 8,000 square feet. Sure enough, she had gotten $20,000 behind and was now in pre-foreclosure. I looked at the balance of the note and saw an opportunity to get the property for approximately $400,000 dollars. The property was worth somewhere in the $700,000 range. The seller wanted $100,000 for her equity, but we agreed on $75,000 minus the price of catching the property up and costs. When I went to the house to have all of the contracts signed, I had a cashier's check in my pocket for her equity totaling $55,000. I had subtracted the $20,000 in back payments I had made directly to the mortgage company. Upon my arrival I saw a large moving van backed up to the front door, and it was at least three quarters of the way full. Inside the house packed boxes were stacked everywhere; the beds were even torn down and leaning against the wall. The seller asked for another forty-eight hours to complete the move. Sure, no problem. And I was right: it was no problem for her, but it was a problem for me. Instead of forty-eight hours, it took almost four months and more money than I want to admit to here. All I had to have done was show her the check and tell her it would be hers as soon as she could give me the keys to her now-vacant home, but *no*—I had to be gullible. Now you know why we have a "cash for KEYS" policy and you should too.

Step 6: Market the Property and Make Some Money

Figure 10-2 is a review of the pre-foreclosure process.

1. Locate a foreclosure listing service to get the information you need.

2. Arrange for private money to be available to stop the foreclosure on the right deal.

3. Mail the pre-foreclosure letter (Figure 10-1).

4. Use the WOW process to gather information from the sellers who call you from the letters.

5. Make an offer. Remember: Do not give anyone any cash until you have a signed contract (purchase and sale agreement), the deed to the property, and the keys to their now vacant property.

6. Market the property.

FIGURE 10-2

And that's what it takes to get you in the pre-foreclosure business.

Chapter Summary

For the real estate investor, foreclosures can be extremely profitable. Even better is the pre-foreclosure market. Not only do you get to help someone before they are financially ruined, you can get in on the market before the house goes into foreclosure. If you follow the process outlined in Figure 10-2 and use the appropriate tools from other chapters, pre-foreclosures can increase your real estate income dramatically.

In the next chapter, I will explain how using "subject to" financing can help you get houses for free.

Pitfalls Recap

FIND THE DOUGH TO MAKE YOUR PRE-FORECLOSURE MACHINE GO!
Know before you ever start your pre-foreclosure marketing machine
that you will have to have some cash.

YOU'D BE LOCO NOT TO GO LOCAL. I believe you will be best served
by using a local service.

STAY AWAY FROM SKINNY DEALS. One of the leading reasons people fail in our business is they jump all over a deal because it's possible and not because it's a good deal.

NOT GETTING ENOUGH INVESTOR CASH TO COVER IT ALL. When you
are agreeing on the amount of money your private investor is going to
put up you must make sure you take everything into consideration.

THE LURE OF THE BIG-DOLLAR HOUSE. High-end homes will put
you out of business in a hurry.

WARNING: THIS IS A DEEP HOLE. Don't ever give any cash out of
your pocket for a deal until you have the keys to their now vacant
house.

WOULD YOU LIKE
A FREE HOUSE?

DO I WANT a *free* house? Who ever heard of such a thing? You must be kidding when you say I can get a *free* house. No, I'm not kidding. It happens all the time in our business. People all across America are giving houses away. In this chapter you're going to learn what I believe to be the single most powerful technique for the creative buying of real estate in existence today: Subject to.

What will you be subjected to using "subject to"? Like most things in life that are great or powerful, this is simple. "Subject to" means we are purchasing the property "subject to" the underlying loan. It works in the same manner as a contingency or subject to appraisal. When an appraiser states that the property's value will be X number of dollars when certain repairs are completed (in other words, "subject to" certain repairs being completed), that is a contingency or subject to appraisal. Any time you are buying a property "subject to," you are simply recognizing the existence of an underlying loan.

You might be thinking, "They can't give me a house if they still have a mortgage on it." That is the conventional way of thinking. It is incorrect. There are two completely separate issues here, and you must be able to understand both of them before we move on. What you must recognize and understand is that you are dealing with two separate components: ownership and liens. Most of us have a hard time separating ownership, which is controlled through the deed, from the mortgage or lien(s) against the property. Let's take a look at each issue.

Ownership of real property or real estate is controlled through a deed. If the deed is put into your name, you own the property. Typically, we have a vision of the deed as some sort of Holy Grail document. This document is passed down from owner to owner, so if a property is very old, the deed is very old. Naturally, we think there can be only one. As in most good myths, there are some grains of truth in our thinking, but it is the rest of the story, as Paul Harvey would say, that makes all the difference. "There can be only one deed" is not entirely correct. Actually, there can only be one deed *in force* at any one time. And the "in force" deed is the last deed recorded. This is a very important issue. For a new deed to be created and then be in force, it must be recorded at the courthouse. For any document to be recorded at the courthouse, it must be notarized.

PITFALL: THE NOSY NOTARY

Over the years I have run into several nosy notaries. There have even been a few cases in which the notary wanted to know what I was doing because he had property he needed to sell. We have to understand the notary's role in this whole process. A notary public is a person commissioned to verify that the signatures on a document or contract are valid. The validity comes from the fact that the notary has checked our government-issued ID or passport verifying that we are who we say we are. Once the notary has established our identity, he witnesses the signing of the document or contract. He is swearing to the fact he saw you actually sign the document or contract in front of him and that the signatures on the document or contract were made by the parties, in this case, the seller and the buyer.

Some notaries feel they need to know what is being signed before they notarize it. *It is none of their business.* The notary public is not verifying the validity of the document or contract or anything said in the contract. He is only verifying that the signatures on the document or contract were made by the parties to the contract.

Once a deed has been filed and recorded at the courthouse, you own the property. You own the property whether there are any liens on it or not. You own the property even if there is an underlying mortgage on the property.

The mortgage or lien does not go away simply because the ownership changed. This change in ownership does not require the approval of the mortgage company or lien holder. Many people get confused here because they mentally cannot separate the ownership of a property from the mortgages or liens on a property. The bulk of this confusion comes from the use of the terms "clean title" and "clear title."

Clear title on a property means the property does not have any liens or mortgages against it. It is short for "free and clear." If a property is free of any liens or mortgages against it, the person listed on the title is the clear owner.

A clean title, on the other hand, simply means that the liens or mortgages on the property have been correctly filed and must be paid before the title can be clear.

You may have heard someone speak of a title having a "cloud" on it. The title can't be clear if it has a cloud on it. A cloud on a title is simply a dispute of some type concerning the property. The dispute could concern ownership of the property, or it could concern a lien or mortgage against the property. Any cloud on a title must be removed before the title becomes clear.

Ownership of the property changes hands through the signing of the deed from the seller to the buyer, which is the important point I wanted to make.

Mortgage

The mortgage, or any other unpaid valid lien, stays with the property until it has been paid or satisfied. Notice I used the term "valid."

PITFALL: A VALID LIEN

For any lien to be valid and enforceable, it must be filed at the courthouse. If you have a lien, do not procrastinate: Get it filed immediately. If you lag on the filing of any lien and the property is sold before you file, you just made a contribution to the seller. It is not the seller's responsibility to file the lien. It is yours. And if a sale is completed before your filing, shame on you.

To recap: All it takes for someone to give me their house is for them to either sign over the existing deed or simply create a new one. Yep, you got it. If you are wondering where you can get a blank deed, go to http://www.AreYouDUMBEnoughToBeRICH.com and click on the menu button marked "Contracts and Forms." You'll see "Blank Sample Deed." Once the deed has been signed and filed at the courthouse, you own the property. There are other documents you will need that are covered in subsequent chapters and in Chapter 22, Pulling It All Together.

You might be wondering whether the owner can give you the house if there is a mortgage on it. Yes. Once the deed is executed, you own the property. Now let's get into what happens with the underlying mortgage.

The underlying mortgage on a "subject to" property will continue to have payments made until you have your buyer refinanced. At the time of this refinancing, the underlying or "Subject mortgage" will be paid off and the clean title will pass to the new buyer, who is your customer.

Once you have purchased a property subject to, you will be making the mortgage payments for a period ranging from one to sixty months. You will be making mortgage payments on a loan that is still in the name of the seller. You will be making mortgage payments that the bank or mortgage company will be happy to accept.

It is time to shift gears for a few minutes and discuss payments on the underlying mortgage. First, let's cover the dreaded "due on sale" clause that exists in every mortgage. There are two sides to the due on sale clause. There is the legal/technical side, and there is the practical side.

The legal/technical side states that if any changes occur in the status of the borrower and/or the property, the mortgage company or bank *has the right to call the loan.* This means that if there has been a sale of the property (and in our case, it has been sold from the seller to us), the mortgage company can say the entire balance is due. Thus the term "due on sale." Make no mistake concerning the due on sale clause: The mortgage company or bank has every legal right to call this loan due. Now let's look at the practical side of the issue.

The practical side of the due on sale clause is this: If the payments on a mortgage issued through a bank or mortgage company are being made on time, every time, the institution has what is called a performing loan. The borrower is performing the way he said he would when he took out the loan. And how do banks and mortgage companies make their money? Through the points on the loan and the interest on the funds loaned by a bank. And through points on the loan and the servicing fee collected each month by the mortgage company. Both the mortgage company and the bank charge points to create a new loan. "Points" is simply an industry term used for the percentage fee charged to originate or create a new loan. To make it less offensive to the borrower, the term "points" is used instead of telling you, "We are going to charge you anywhere from 1 to 5 percent of the amount of the loan just to do the paperwork." Mortgage companies also charge a monthly fee for what is called the "servicing" of the note.

The servicing of a note is mostly the collection of the monthly payments. At the time of this writing, most mortgage companies are receiving approximately $7.50 per month per loan payment to service the account. It doesn't sound like a lot of money until you begin to think about the number of mortgages created in the United States each month. This applies to all the existing loans as well. Literally millions and millions of loans are creating a $7.50 fee each and every month. It seems logical therefore to assume that, if a bank or mortgage company makes their money from the interest earned on a loan and from the servicing fee created each month and if they have a performing loan, they would not want to call the loan due. They have enough property they have had to foreclose on already, and they don't need any more. Contrary to what most homeowners, especially those who are in danger of foreclosure, think, the bank or mortgage company does not want their house. They are *not* trying to steal the owner's hard-earned equity. They just want the payments made and made on time, every time.

There is more to this practical side of subject to. Let's think about the handling process for a single payment. First we need to look at who's posting our payments on the loan. Do you think it's the head of the legal department who says, "Wait a minute here, the person who sent us this payment is not the person whose name is on the loan. Oh my gosh, it's being made by a company. This has to stop now. We are going to call this loan due, and I'm not going to pay any attention to the fact these payments are being made on time, every time."? That's not the way it happens. Our payment arrives at the bank or mortgage company, the envelope is opened, and the check is forwarded to a data entry clerk. In my case, these subject to payments are made with no payment coupon included. What does the data entry clerk need to be able to post a payment? He needs the loan number to appear on the check and the check to be made out in the correct amount. OK, so our payment arrives, it's opened, and this one check with no payment coupon is sitting in front of a data entry clerk ready for posting. By the way, what do you think this data entry person is being paid—$6, $8, maybe $10 an hour? Our heroic data entry clerk now looks at the check and the only information he has to work with is the fact that we put the loan number in the memo section of the check—please remember to do that. Looking at the loan number, the data entry clerk pulls up the account and sees that the payment amount on the check and the loan information all match, and our check is deposited faster than you can say "due on sale clause." And that, my friend, is the practical side of the due on sale clause.

The banks and mortgage companies are aware of the fact that they are setting a legal precedent by accepting these payments. With regard to this point, be aware that mortgages now contain a waiver clause. This waiver clause states that just because they have been accepting your payments doesn't mean they can't change their minds if they want to and call the loan. This is to cover their legal assets (no pun intended). Just remember that it is in the bank's or mortgage company's best interest to accept our payments and not call the loan due.

PITFALL: TIMELY PAYMENTS

If you are buying a property subject to and you start having to make payments on the underlying mortgage, do not allow any of those payments to be late. They *must* be on time.

This is a good time to make sure you understand that when we buy a property subject to, we are not assuming any legal responsibility for the repayment of the debt. We are simply servicing (making the payments on) the debt.

How do I as a new investor write a contract subject to? In each and every real estate contract, you will find a section for the price. You can't write a contract without the price, right? What we are going to do here is a little different. Instead of the price being a number, we are going to write "a description of the price." Let's look at an example. The description of the price in a subject to contract would read as follows:

> The total purchase price is: The balance of the mortgage held at [insert the name of the mortgage company here] loan number [insert the loan account number here] for the property located at [insert the

street address and legal description here] created in the name of [insert the name of the seller here], AT THE TIME LOAN NUMBER [insert the loan account number] IS PAID IN FULL.

If there were any cash going to the seller for this purchase, you would add the following phrase prior to the price description as follows:

$5,000.00 cash (Five Thousand Dollars Cash) and the balance of the mortgage held at [insert the name of the mortgage company here] loan number [insert the loan account number here] for the property located at [insert the street address and legal description here] created in the name of [insert the name of the seller here], AT THE TIME LOAN NUMBER [insert the loan account number] IS PAID IN FULL.

This last sentence is very important. The phrase, AT THE TIME LOAN NUMBER (insert the loan account number) IS PAID IN FULL could put several thousand extra dollars in your pocket. Any time you are buying a property subject to, it becomes likely you will end up making a mortgage payment or two. Any time payments are made on a loan, the balance of the principal is reduced. Depending on the age of the loan, the principal reduction could very small or very nice. Whatever the amount, we want to receive credit for the principal reduction. Each and every payment made makes the equity in the property grow. It may grow a little or it may grow a lot, but it will grow. We want the equity growth to be for us and not for the seller. If you use the phrasing listed above as you write a subject to contract, the additional equity will end up in your bank account.

Chapter Summary

Do I want a *free* house? Who ever heard of such a thing? You are kidding when you say I can get a *free* house? No, I'm not kidding, it happens all the time in our business. So now you see that if you purchase a house subject to and if there is no equity involved for the seller, you are getting a "free" house. You haven't made a down payment. You haven't had to go to the bank or mortgage company and take out a mortgage. In many cases the seller has walked away from their equity just for the debt relief you can provide them.

My attorney friends ask me to be sure to remind you that there needs to some type of monetary exchange for a contract to be binding if it were ever challenged in court. This exchange can be as little as $100.00. This will always be the safest way to go.

In the next chapter we are going to get into how you get paid to buy a house. Is that something you'd be interested in? Turn the page and let's get started.

Pitfalls Recap

THE NOSEY NOTARY. The notary public is not verifying the validity of the document or contract or anything said in the contract. They are only verifying that the signatures on the document or contract were made by the parties to the contract.

TIMELY PAYMENTS. Any time you are buying a property subject to and you start having to make payments on the underlying mortgage whatever you do, do not allow any of those payments to be late. They *must* be on time.

A VALID LIEN. For any lien to be valid and enforceable it MUST be filed at the courthouse.

GETTING PAID
TO BUY A HOUSE

NOW YOU know how to get a free house. Would you like to take that concept one step farther? How would you like to get paid to take a house? I bet you think I've gone off the deep end. What would ever cause someone to pay you to buy their house?

There are circumstances every day where people need to get rid of a piece of property and are willing to pay us to make it happen. I'm not talking about someone who is desperate and needs to sell in the worst way. Many people have very little equity in their home and then decide they want or need to sell it.

You will never get paid to take a house if you do not *ask*. A wonderful lesson in life came from my dad. He said, "Just ask, all they can do is say *no*. They can't shoot you and eat you." The worst thing that's going to happen is that the seller is going to say no. I can promise you this: No one will ever pay you to take a house if you do not ask.

PITFALL: I KNOW HOW THEY FEEL

Here is a conceptual statement that is very important to your success in the business. Everyone does not value real estate the same way we do. There's a revelation to you. Just because we feel real estate is the best place to make money on God's green earth doesn't mean everyone feels the same way. Your business is going to run a lot more smoothly, and you'll keep from pulling your hair out if you just understand and accept this basic truth. We do not know how other people feel or what is going on in their lives, and therefore we can never prejudge another person.

So how does this phenomenon of being paid to buy a house happen? In the last chapter we established the ability to buy a property "subject to" where the underlying loan stays intact. We are going to build on this principle. If we are buying property using the seller's credit, which is all buying subject to is, is it such a far stretch for you to believe we can take the principle to the next level?

Let's take a look at how we can position ourselves to have someone pay us to buy their house. When we are offering to buy someone's house as a "subject to" agreement, we simply need to ask them this, "I need you to help me with the marketing of this house. You're probably wondering what you could do. The only way I see I can make this property work is for you pay the next four payments after I take possession of the property." "What? You must be crazy. Why would I do such a thing?" says the seller.

And now we build our logical case for the seller's paying us to take their house. You should say, "Look, I know that may sound a little strange to you, but let's look at what it's going to cost you if I don't buy your house.

"If I don't buy your house, is it fair to think you're probably going to list the property with a real estate agent? Many people feel they could sell their home themselves only to list it with a real estate agent after months of hassle and frustration and still not having the house sold. When you use a real estate agent to sell your property, you're going to incur some basic costs, right? I just call it the 'cost of selling your house.' Many people do not look at the details of selling their house when they decide to move. They know what they want to sell the house for, and they subtract the balance of their mortgage and, presto, they know how much profit or equity they have. *Wrong!* These people are not taking into consideration things like closing costs. Did you know closing costs nationally run between 2 and 3 percent of the total sales price? So let's do the math. [At this point I ask the seller to write the numbers down, and we calculate the numbers together.] You want to sell your house for $300,000. Therefore $300,000 times 3 percent closing cost is $9,000. How long do you think it might take you to sell your property?"

Whatever they answer, I respond with, "The national average is around six months to sell a listed property. During the time it takes to sell your property, will you be living in the house or do need to move sooner?"

Many times the seller will need to move prior to the selling of the property, which means the seller will be making two house payments until the property is sold. "Mr. or Ms. Seller, would you agree that six months is a reasonable amount of time to sell your home? You are not going to be living in the property for six months, but you are still going to have to make payments. Since you still have to make the payments, you will need to put the total of those payments into your 'cost of sale' calculation. OK, six payments at $2,000 per month is a total of $12,000. And we can't forget the real estate agent's commission either. The average commission in most parts of the country is 6 percent. If we take 6 percent of $300,000, we get $18,000." Now we are going to total all of this up and see our total cost of sales.

In no particular order the cost would be:

Real estate agent's commission $=$ **$18,000** **(6 percent × $300,000)**	
Closing cost of 3 percent $=$ **$9,000** **(3 percent × $300,000)**	
Six months of payments $=$ **$12,000** **(6 × $2,000)**	
TOTAL COST OF SALE **$39,000**	

For the sake of argument, we'll say the seller has a really good real estate agent, and the sale can be completed in half the time or ninety days. The total cost of sale would still be $33,000. Taking this amount from the sale price reduces the check at closing to $267,000. Most people do not realize that these costs need to go into their cost of sale calculation. Please note that we are basing this example on the seller's receiving a full-price offer on the property, which doesn't always happen.

At this point, we have agreed it will cost something for the seller to sell this property. Then we say, "If you sell in ninety days, we have agreed the cost of sale will be $33,000. Of course, Mr. or Ms. Seller, you do realize the selling process could be much longer? If your selling time is as short as ninety days, the cost will still dramatically affect your net proceeds, and you have all those real estate agents and their clients traipsing through your home. So now you've got to keep it in showing condition all the time since you never know when a real estate agent is going to call." I then say, "Of course, there is a simpler and much less expensive answer to this process—you put all of the traditional mess associated with selling your home behind you. I am your answer to the sale of your house today. I can do this much more cheaply. We agreed on a cost of sale of $33,000 if everything went very quickly. I can resolve all of those inconveniences we discussed for approximately one third of what it could cost you to sell your home through a traditional sale. I'll buy your home today, and you can get on with your life, and this house will be behind you."

Here is where I would go into the Cafeteria Close or A, B, C offers. (Making multiple offers is covered in detail in Chapter 13.) "This is a beautiful home you have. Let me jot down some ways I could purchase your home and get this wrapped up for you quickly and easily. First, I agree your home has a market value of $300,000, and I might be able to pay you the full asking price for your house. Would that be of interest to you?" "Yes, of course it would," replies the seller. "OK, give me a minute here to put a pencil to this."

Now I write out the A, B, C offers.

OFFER A: $300,000 TODAY. I will purchase the property from you for $300,000 with your underlying mortgage of $208,000 staying intact until I successfully market the property. There will be a 36-month balloon note or maximum time frame for me to sell the property. I retain the right to have the property occupied by a tenant/buyer while I work with my tenant/buyer to get them refinanced. At the time of my tenant/buyer's new loan, the remaining balance of your mortgage will be paid off. I will guarantee the maintenance and start making payments 120 days after taking possession. During my 32-month payment period (36 months–120 days) I will pay to your escrow agent the amount of $2,625 per month. This amount is to cover all mortgage payments, the monthly insurance payment, and the monthly taxes. (The $2,625 per month more than covers a $300,000 note at 6 percent interest plus yearly taxes of $7,500 and yearly insurance of $2,250, which comes to $2,611.15.)

At this point I will say, "This puts your cost of sale at approximately $8,000—one fourth of the traditional cost without all of the hassles. I know you're probably concerned about your ability to get a new mortgage if the old one is still in your name. There are a few basic steps here. Keeping the existing mortgage can improve your ability to get a new loan. By completing a purchase and sales agreement we have now created a receivable note for you. This receivable note offsets your existing mortgage note 100 percent, and it will even put some additional cash in your pocket. Based on our earlier conversation [when we asked the WOW questions], you said the existing note had a payment of $2,000 per month, which included your taxes and insurance, is that correct? I could pay you $2,625 per month until I get the property sold. That's an extra $625 per month, which is credited to your income. Basically, you just got a raise. That raise will improve your ability to get another loan. Do you see how that works?"

PITFALL: THE SAME MORTGAGE COMPANY RED FLAG

Any time I am purchasing a house "subject to," I want to send the seller to my mortgage broker and not have them go back to the mortgage company from which they got their existing mortgage. The reason here is very simple: If they go back to the same mortgage company, it could create *red flags* or questions about the sale which most sellers aren't capable of answering. This could in turn cause the mortgage company to call the loan even though they are getting monthly payments on time. Also, not being able to answer these questions quickly and easily can lead to confusion, and a confused mind says *no*. Our seller is likely to get frustrated when they can't quickly and easily explain what they are doing with us, and they begin to worry they aren't going to get their new loan, and the entire deal could fall apart here. How do we handle this? We help the seller by having the following conversation with them at the time we are presenting the A, B, C offers.

"With all of the mortgage programs existing today, I could introduce you to my mortgage broker if you wish. He does an excellent job for my clients and could probably get you the lowest possible rate on your new loan. Would you like for me to do that for you?" We are accomplishing several things here: First, we have increased their cash flow, which improves their financial statement. Second, we are providing them with an excellent source of financing, and third we are keeping them from being in a position where they are trying to explain our business to a third party.

OFFER B: $255,000 TODAY. I will purchase the property from you for $25,000 cash with the remainder of the purchase price to be carried by you until I successfully market the property. The $25,000 payment to be made on or before _____, 200X with a 36-month balloon note or maximum time frame for me to sale the property. I retain the right to have the property occupied by a tenant/buyer while I work with said tenant/buyer to get them refinanced. At the time of my tenant/buyer's new loan, the remaining balance of your mortgage will be paid off. I will guarantee the maintenance and start making the payments thirty days after taking possession. During my 36-month payment period I will pay to your escrow agent the amount of $2,200 per month. This amount is to cover all mortgage payments, the monthly insurance payment, and the monthly taxes. This offer gives you $25,000 now and an *extra* monthly check of $200 per month. You have additional funds for the down payment on your new home and increased monthly income to make qualifying easier.

OFFER C: $210,000 ALL CASH and close by [30 days from the date of the contract].

You're probably wondering where you are going to get the money if they agree to this offer. Go back to your private investor script because that's where you are going to get the money from. It is also where you are going to get the money if the seller accepts offer B.

Do not be surprised if the seller accepts the all-cash offer. If you're surprised, you're trying to think for the seller and you *can't.* If the seller accepts the all-cash offer, they would have the property out of their name now, but would receive the least amount of money. I have had this happen before, so don't be surprised.

Then, to make sure I am covered legally, I say, "Of course, Mr. and Ms. Seller, all offers are subject to having the property inspected and appraised at my expense."

Whichever offer is accepted, I am going to sell the property in the same manner: lease–purchase option with no bank qualifying. I'll set the price at a minimum of $325,000, which is above the current market value of the house. By offering the no bank qualifying, I can get this top-dollar price. I will be looking for a down payment from $15,000 to $25,000, which is reasonable for this price of a home. For the sake of this example, let's agree the down payment is $20,000 and see how it works with each of our original offers to the seller.

Chapter Summary

If you purchased the home with offer A, you have no down payment on the property, but you have a payment of $2,625 going to the seller. Our buyer has given us a down payment of $20,000, and their payment to us is based on a thirty-year loan at 9 3/4 percent, which creates a payment of $3,432.92 and does include our buyer's taxes and insurance payment. We are paying out $2,625 to the seller and pocketing the monthly difference of $807.92 per month. If we are able to get our buyer refinanced into their own mortgage within eighteen months, we will have received $14,542.56 in monthly spread money and a small check at the time of our buyer's refinancing of approximately $5,000. The total approximate profit of this deal is $39,542.56, and all we have in the deal is the $100.00 binder or escrow we paid the seller at the time we signed the contract.

If we purchased the home with offer B, we have now paid a down payment of $25,000 on the property (which we received from a private investor at 10 percent until the time when our buyer is refinanced) and a monthly payment of $2,200 going to the seller. Our buyer has given us a down payment of $20,000, and their payment to us is based on a thirty-year loan at 9 3/4 percent loan, creating a payment of $3,432.92 that includes our buyer's taxes and insurance payment. We are paying out $2,200 to the seller and pocketing the monthly difference of $1,232.92 per month. If we are able to get our buyer refinanced into their own mortgage within eighteen months, we will have received $22,192.56 in monthly spread money and a big check at the time of our buyer's refinancing of approximately $46,250. This $46,250 check is *after* the title company has paid our private investor their $25,000 and 10 percent interest or $28,750. The total approximate profit on this deal is $88,442.56, and all we have in the deal is the $100.00 binder or escrow and the private investor's funds of $25,000 we paid the seller at the time we signed the contract.

If we purchased the home with offer C, we paid $210,000 cash, which we received from our private investor. The $210,000 will accrue simple interest at 10 percent per year for the next two years. Two years gives us enough time to market the property and give our buyer the previously stated eighteen months to get refinanced. Our buyer has given us a down payment of $20,000 and their payment to us is based on a thirty-year loan at 9 3/4 percent loan, which creates a payment of $3,432.92 and includes our buyer's taxes and insurance payment. We are paying out $1,750 to our private investor in a monthly interest expense and pocketing the monthly difference of $1,682.92 If we are able to get our buyer refinanced into their own mortgage within eighteen months, we will have received $30,292.56 in monthly spread money and a big check at the time of our buyer's refinancing of approximately $95,000. The total approximate profit on this deal is $145,292.56 and all we have in the deal is the $100.00 binder or escrow and the private investor's funds of $210,000 we paid the seller at the time we closed on the purchase.

Remember that the interest for the private investor was paid monthly so all we had to pay at the time of the buyer's refinancing was the principal balance of $210,000.

There is so much in these last two chapters it would do your investing career good to go back and reread both of them.

Pitfalls Recap

I KNOW HOW THEY FEEL. Everyone does not value real estate the same way we do. Just because we feel real estate is the best place to make money on God's green earth doesn't mean everyone feels the same way. We do not know how other people feel or what is going on in their lives, and therefore we can never prejudge another person.

THE SAME MORTGAGE COMPANY RED FLAG. Any time I am purchasing a house "subject to," I want to send the seller to my mortgage broker and not have them go back to the mortgage company from which they got their existing mortgage.

MAKING
MULTIPLE OFFERS
PICK AN OFFER, ANY OFFER

THIS CHAPTER is about constructing offers for a house where you allow the seller to pick the answer that best meets their personal needs. Whichever offer they chose earns you a profit. Any answer they choose will let you make a *big fat deposit* to your bank account. Don't you just love making deposits? I know I do, especially *big fat deposits*. Those are the ones where you see the teller's eyes widen as they think to themselves, "What does this guy do for a living? Whatever it is, it can't be legal." The ability to make more than one offer to a seller and to help solve their problem will greatly improve the number of deals you successfully close.

MULTIPLE OFFERS WORKSHEET

Property: _____

_____

OFFER A = Seller's asking price with the seller carrying all of the financing, as long as the seller's asking price isn't <u>above</u> the market value.

OFFER B: Is the split offer between A and C:

    Offer A – 15% – any cash required by the seller. With the seller carrying the rest of the financing.

OFFER C = Cash Offer = Comps – (30 percent of the comps) – Cost of repairs.

FIGURE 13-1

Figuring Out What to Offer

Take a piece of paper and write the letters A, B, C vertically down the left-hand side, leaving several lines of space between each letter. This will become your offer worksheet (see Figure 13-1); it will be the model you use on a go-forward basis. *All three* of the offers you are going to construct will be given to the seller at the same time. This offer sheet will not be a contract but simply a way for the seller to see all that you have to offer. Once the seller decides which offer is best for them, all they need to do is initial the offer they prefer, and then you can draw up the contract.

Here's how to figure out what your A-B-C offers will be. Your "A" offer will be a full asking price offer. Obviously if you paid every seller their full asking price with nothing in return you wouldn't be able to buy very many houses. That's why we have to make sure we are getting something in return.

Remember that there are only two things you have to negotiate in real estate: price and terms. If you are paying full price, then the terms should be in your favor. If the seller is receiving full price, then you should receive full carry. In other words the seller has to provide you with 100 percent of the seller financing. Most sellers will not know how to do this. It is up to you to show the seller how to provide owner financing.

The "A" in the A offer stands for "all." The seller is carrying *all* of the financing, which means the mortgage stays in their name.

PITFALL: THE SELLER'S BIG FEAR

Most sellers will ask, "Won't this prevent me from buying another house if my underlying mortgage on this house is still in my name?" And the answer is *no,* not as long as you provide the seller with a "purchase and sale agreement." The purchase and sale agreement shows that you have bought the property from the seller. The seller can sell you his or her house without the underlying loan being paid off, and you can buy it without paying off the underlying loan. For those of you possessing a working knowledge of basic real estate transactions, you may be wondering about the due on sale clause* contained in most mortgages. Mortgage underwriters look at the purchase and sale agreement (the contract) on the existing house as an income-producing contract for you, the seller. This income provides a way to wash out or equalize the debt obligation created by the original mortgage. This wash-out or equalization allows the seller to qualify for his or her new loan as if the old one doesn't exist. By the time you have finished this book you will be very comfortable dealing with the due on sale clause.

PITFALL: THE TWO-MORTGAGE DILEMMA[†]

Please note that there is a sidebar to consider here: If the seller goes back to his or her original mortgage company to secure the funding for their new house, this will not work. You must advise the seller to go to a different mortgage company for the new loan. This keeps any red flags from popping up about the original mortgage and its due on sale clause.

Next we are going to move to our C offer. Once we have completed the C offer, you will see (no pun intended) why we create the C offer second, even though it will appear last on our offer sheet. The "C" in our C offer stands for "cash." This will be our all-cash offer. As Ron LeGrand once said to me, "If you're not concerned the seller may cuss you out when they see your all-cash offer, well it's simply too high an offer."

---

* For a review of "due on sale," see pp. 110–111.

† See also Pitfall, pp. 120–121.

PITFALL: THE EMBARRASSMENT FACTOR

As a new investor, many of you will allow your personal feelings of embarrassment to cloud your judgment. What I mean by that statement is that you may feel uncomfortable making offer C. Because is it low, you will prejudge the seller's response and cost yourself thousands and thousands of dollars in the course of your investing career. It will also significantly shorten your real estate investment career. For all of you I do have an answer: Each time you feel your hands starting to sweat because you're about to make a low all-cash offer, look in the mirror with all of the conviction you can muster and say, "Get over it!" Never forget that you are *not* trying to decide for the seller what is best for them. You are offering three solutions to their problem and letting them decide what is in their best interest.

Back to our C offer: There is a formula you can use to safely arrive at an all-cash number.

The all-cash formula is created by first determining what the current market value of the property would be if it were in excellent condition. Again, there is only one way to do this. You need to get "comps" or comparable sales.

Comps are best created by a real estate agent or broker. Comps are the closed sales of other "comparable" houses in the same neighborhood. Comps only look at sales of homes of a similar size that are in a similar condition and are in a similar, if not the same, neighborhood. Comps in almost all cases should be no older than six months. If the real estate agent needs to go back more than six months to be able to establish comps, it is probably either because the property is in an isolated area or because it is a high-end property. The larger the market value of the property, the harder it is to establish good comps.

The C offer is established by subtracting 30 percent from the market value of the property. The 30 percent number covers two critical areas of our business, *profit* and *contingencies.*

Your profit on any property should be no less than 20 percent. Your time is too valuable for you to work for less than 20 percent. And yes, I am talking about 20 percent of the total value of the property, which is 20 percent of what the property is sold for. There are exceptions, but not many.

Please do not allow yourself to get into a bad deal just because you were too impatient to wait for the right deal to show up.

> **Remember: You will never go broke over**
> **the deal you didn't do.**

PITFALL: DEAL-ITIS

There is a condition that I call "deal-itis." Its symptoms are easy to spot. They start with an anemic bank account and slowly drain the life out of an investor. The cure for deal-itis is simple. It starts when we administer a shot of profit into our business.

There is a world of common sense in this statement. Allowing yourself to work for less than 20 percent on a deal such as a rehabilitation that takes up a lot of your time will quickly put an end to your investing career.

PITFALL: NO SURPRISE FACTOR

It is rare in our business to complete a transaction with no surprises along the way. The professional term for surprises is contingencies. The remaining 10 percent you are deducting in your all-cash offer is to cover any surprises or contingencies.

To complete the cash offer, you will need to deduct the cost of any needed repairs from the number. The formula will now look like this:

$200,000 **Market value of the property**
– 60,000 **30 percent (20 percent profit and 10 percent for contingencies)**
$140,000 **Maximum offer if no repairs are needed (minus any needed repairs)**

Now you have two of the three offers completed. The A offer is for the full market value of the property with the seller carrying all of the financing. The C offer is an all-cash offer.

The B offer is our "split-funded" offer. Split funding simply means we are going to split our A and C offers by giving the seller some cash and requiring the seller to carry the remaining financing.

In many cases the seller will tell you they are open to carrying some of the financing, but they want you (the buyer) to have some money in the deal. They want you to have something at risk. They are putting up their real estate and now require you to put up some cash. For our example, the seller wants us to put up at least 10 percent or $20,000 in cash. Here's what our B—split-funded—offer looks like:

A offer is $200,000
C offer is $140,000

MULTIPLE OFFERS SHEET

To: John and Mary Owner   **From:** Bill Barnett

In regards to your property located at _____, I would like to make the following offers:

Offer A: $200,000. I will purchase the property from you for $200,000 with your underlying mortgage of $128,000 staying intact until I successfully market the property. There will be a 36-month balloon note or maximum time frame for me to sale sell the property. I retain the right to have the property occupied by my tenant/buyer while I work with my tenant/buyer to get them refinanced. At the time of my tenant/buyer's new loan, the remaining balance of your mortgage will be paid off along with the remaining balance of the $72,000 second mortgage. I will guarantee the maintenance and start making payments 90 days after taking possession. During my 33-month payment period (36 months minus 90 days), I will pay to your escrow agent the amount of $1,700 per month. This amount is to cover the $1,300 payment on first mortgage, the monthly insurance payment, monthly taxes, and $400 toward the second mortgage.

Offer B: $170,000. "Split Funded." I will purchase the property from you for $170,000 with your underlying mortgage of $128,000 staying intact until I successfully market the property. There will be a $20,000 payment on or before _____, 200X and a 36-month balloon note or maximum time frame for me to sell the property. I retain the right to have the property occupied by my tenant/buyer while I work with said tenant/buyer to get them refinanced. At the time of my tenant/buyer's new loan, the remaining balance of your mortgage will be paid off along with the remaining balance of the $22,000 second mortgage. I will guarantee the maintenance and start making the payments 90 days after taking possession. During my 33-month

FIGURE 13-2

payment period (36 months minus 90 days), I will pay to your escrow agent the amount of $1,550 per month. This amount is to cover the $1,300 payment on the first mortgage, the monthly insurance payment, monthly taxes, and $250 toward the second mortgage.

Offer C: $140,000. All Cash. Close by 200X.

All offers are subject to having the property inspected and appraised at my expense. Please feel free to initial the offer you prefer.

Regards,

Bill Barnett

The B offer will split these two offers and will be $170,000. This figure is arrived at by subtracting the C offer of $140,000 from the A offer of $200,000, leaving us with $60,000. Take the $60,000 and split it in two. We are now dealing with $30,000 that you add to the C offer. $140,000 plus $30,000 equals $170,000. From this $170,000 the seller wants to receive $20,000 in cash. Our B offer now shows the seller receiving $20,000 in cash and carrying the balance of the offer $150,000 (170,000 − 20,000 = 150,000). We now have all three of the offers. Figure 13-2 is a sample of my offers sheet containing all three offers. Remember, they are all made at the same time.

You will never go broke over the deal you didn't do.

Chapter Summary

Making multiple offers is one way to increase the odds of closing a deal. You are giving the seller options, so they are more likely to choose what works for them. At the same time, every offer works for you and puts money in your bank account. Use the worksheet and sample offer letter to create multiple offers for your next property.

Pitfalls Recap

THE SELLER'S BIG FEAR: THE TWO-MORTGAGE DILEMMA. Most sellers will ask, "Won't this prevent me from buying another house if my underlying mortgage on this house is still in my name?" And the answer is no, not as long as you provide the seller with a "purchase and sale agreement." You must advise the seller to go to a different mortgage company for the new loan.

THE EMBARRASSMENT FACTOR. You may feel uncomfortable making a low offer. Because is it low, you will prejudge the seller's response and cost yourself thousands and thousands of dollars in the course of your investing career. You are offering three solutions to their problem and letting them decide what is in their best interest.

DEAL-ITIS. Your profit on any property should be no less than 20 percent. Your time is too valuable for you to work for less than 20 percent. And yes, I am talking about 20 percent of the total value of the property, which is 20 percent of what the property is sold for.

NO SURPRISE FACTOR. It is rare in our business to complete a transaction with no surprises along the way. The professional term for surprises is contingencies. The remaining 10 percent you are deducting in your all-cash offer is to cover any surprises or contingencies.

GENERATING
A QUICK SALE
I GOT 'EM, NOW HOW
DO I GET RID OF THEM?

WHEN SELLING a property, there is a wonderful "trade secret" I'd like to now pass along to you. It is a very simple way to set yourself up so that you can easily work with agents. It's your neighborhood home improvement store. No, you can't buy a good real estate broker or agent from such a store, but you may be able to buy the next best thing: a lockbox.

Setting Yourself Up with a Lockbox

Lockboxes are the boxes that hang from the doorknobs of properties listed by real estate agents and brokers. At the time of this writing, lockboxes cost less than fifty dollars.

There are two reasons you want to handle your locks in this manner. First, and this is very subtle, you want to have realtors bringing you potential buyers. The great thing about buyers that are brought to you by real estate agents and brokers is that they are usually cash buyers. Lockboxes allow realtors access to your property that they wouldn't have otherwise. When a top-notch broker or agent sees a lockbox on a property, they know the property is probably owned by an investor.

Simply having the lockbox on the door will make your phone start to ring. The agents and brokers will see it and call. Many of the calls will be to list your property on the multiple listing service (MLS). Once this question has been asked all you need to do is respond with, "I don't list my properties, but I will gladly *protect* your commission if you bring me a buyer. I'll give you the combo to the box if you think you'd like to show the property."

Second, using a lockbox will take the hassle out of selling. This happens because you are able to show the property without having to be there yourself. This will save you tons of time and frustration.

I'm sure you're wondering about security and thinking things will get stolen. Yes, there may be thefts. In the seven plus years I have been doing this business, I've had two theft problems. One was a break-in at the start of a new rehab project where a couple hundred dollars worth of tools were stolen. These petty thieves had kicked in a side door to the garage to gain entry to the house. (I had marked the side door for replacement because it didn't look very secure. Don't you hate being right?)

PITFALL: TOO LAZY TO PACK UP AT THE END OF THE DAY? IT'LL COST YOU!

If you are using a general contractor or a handyman, make sure to have them take all of their tools with them at the end of the day. This may seem like common sense, but many contractors will grow comfortable at your job site and start to leave tools around. If your contractors want to make a contribution to the local Petty Thieves Union, just tell them to leave a case of beer outside the back door. Don't tempt the locals to break in to your house to steal tools. The theft of a few tools, of course, is not the real issue here. The real issue is any damage that may be done to the interior of your rehab while the criminals are inside.

There is also the danger that one of the criminals will get hurt while breaking in and sue you for the injury. This kind of thing has actually happened.

The second break-in occurred at a completed rehab site. A prospective buyer had called inquiring about the property. I gladly gave her the lockbox combination and invited her to see the interior of the house. After a few minutes she called back and asked me to come to the house because the front door was wide open. I left the office to make sure everything was OK for the woman to go inside. When I got to the house, I noticed she had not told me everything. The front door was not wide open—*it wasn't there!* It seems someone in the neighborhood needed a new stove and had mistaken me for Santa Claus. Further investigation revealed that the front door had been removed to allow for easier exit with the stove. The front door was, however, leaning against an interior wall of the living room. Thank you, thieves. The criminals had broken a window to gain access to the property. I wonder why they just didn't call me for the lockbox code.

Please note, neither of these break-ins had anything to do with the lockboxes. Both were forced-entry break-ins. These two break-ins cost me less than $500 total, a small price to pay for all the time I've saved having lockboxes.

I do have to tell you a short story that happened to a friend of mine. You must put this in the proper prospective and realize this is the only time I've ever heard of this happening, and I deal with investors from all over the country every week. It seems someone had called and gotten the lockbox code to one of his properties. Apparently this prospective buyer loved the home but just couldn't afford it. So what would a really creative person do? Just move in, of course. Yep, this person got the code and moved into the house over the weekend. It took my friend several weeks to get this person out of the house. Do not think you can just show up and forcibly remove them from your house.

How to Find Buyers

TAKE OUT AN AD IN THE CLASSIFIEDS. Classifieds have always worked well for me. You do not have to buy large ads with lots of words and lines. What I want an ad to do is make the phone ring. Many of the sales ads I run are "blind" ads. These are ads that do not specifically feature a particular house. The ad placed in the local newspapers reads like this:

> Southwest, Fort Worth
> 2 Executive Homes
> Owner Finance Avail.
> Some Credit Required
> Barnett.PropertyFast.net
> (817) 555–1212

Again, all I'm looking for here is to make the phone ring with prospective buyers. There are two reasons we want to get these calls coming in: First, of course, we are trying to sell the house. Second, we have the ability to create a buyers' list.

CREATE A BUYERS' LIST. Advertising allows us to gather information about people who are looking for a home. Every time somebody calls from one of your ads, it is vital that you record their contact information. You'll need to know the obvious contact information, but you'll also want to ask a few additional questions like:

- Is this the area of town you want to live in?

- How much of a down payment do you have available for your next home?

- What is the maximum amount you are willing to pay monthly?

- What size home are you looking for?

Creating a buyers' list with this information will allow you to buy houses knowing you have several prospective buyers for the property immediately. This will keep your holding cost down. Remember, holding cost is the number-one avoidable expense in your business. Believe me, I know about holding cost and what it can do to your profit margin.

BUY A SIGN. The cheapest form of advertising you will ever have is a sign in the yard saying "FOR SALE BY OWNER." These signs can be bought for less than $20 each. Put out more than one sign to make it more noticeable. No, you aren't going to put out more than one "For Sale By Owner" sign, but do put more than one sign in the yard. Additional signs might read, "Owner Financing Available" or "No Bank Qualifying." Remember learning about buying property "subject to" in Chapter 11. Subject to is how we are able to sell property offering owner financing. Depending on the price of the home, you could put additional signs that read "Rent to Own" or "Lease Purchase Option." If the home is the average home for your area, you may want to use "Rent to Own," and if it is an upper-priced home, use "Lease Purchase Option."

So your multiple signs or sign grouping may look like this for one house: For Sale By Owner, Owner Financing Available, No Bank Qualifying, and We BUY Houses Cash. Believe me, putting up four signs in the same yard attracts attention.

PITFALL: KNOW THE RULES ABOUT SIGNS

Be aware of what the signage rules and regulations are for the neighborhood you're selling in. If you are selling in an upper-priced neighborhood, there may be restrictions about the number of signs that can be in a yard at any one time. This is one of the many drawbacks to upper-priced homes. If you need to order your real estate signs, check out the "Signage Link" at www.AreYou DUMBEnoughToBeRICH.com.

START YOUR OWN WEB SITE. A personal real estate Web site will generate several easy sales per year for you. In the next chapter, I'll show you how easy and inexpensive it is to set up and host your very own real estate Web site.

SEND OUT DIRECT MAIL/FLYERS. They are an excellent way to market your homes. Many home buyers are referred to a neighborhood or particular home by someone they know who already lives in the same subdivision. Don't forget that you can easily get a mortgage broker or title company to share the very low cost of printing and distributing flyers simply by allowing them to put their message on the other side of the flyer. I use this technique a lot.

TRY USING ROUND ROBIN AUCTIONS. These were first applied to real estate sales in the late eighties and early nineties by a man named William G. Effros.

Effros built a complete auction selling system that he detailed fully in his book, *How To Sell Your Home in 5 Days*. In the book Effros describes how he started auctioning off homes in a five-day round robin process. Here's a quick overview.

First, a great deal of interest for the property is created by running an ad stating that the property will be sold to the highest bidder, and the bidding will start at _____. The blank is filled with a number that is so low it represents approximately 50 percent of the market value of the home. This ad is run the three days prior to the auction and the two weekend days when the property is open for viewing. If the minimum number of potential buyers, which is forty, have not called to inquire about the auction in the three days (Wednesday, Thursday, and Friday) prior to the sale, the auction is cancelled.

However, if the minimum number of bidders is reached, you will hold an open house for a few hours on Saturday and Sunday *only*. No one can see the property prior to the viewing times. There are no exceptions. As the prospective bidders come through the property, you will provide them with a complete packet of information on the property.

If you have ever been to a charity silent auction, this process is very similar. As far as property auctions go, this is not your parents' auction. The bidders come through the property and place their bid on an open bid sheet for everyone else to see. The idea here is to create a bidding frenzy, much like what we see on eBay every day. At the close of the viewing hours, you call each of the bidders (hence the round robin) to tell them what the high bid is and to give them an opportunity to increase their bid.

It is a simple and effective system. If you cannot quickly sell a home using the many different ways listed above, the book *How To Sell Your Home in 5 Days* will tell you how to use auctions to your benefit.

Chapter Summary

1. Get lockboxes for each of your properties.

2. Build a working relationship with each of the Realtors calling to list the property by protecting their selling commission if they bring you a cash buyer.

3. Use the tried and true classifieds to sell and collect information about prospective buyers.

4. Build a buyers' list from everyone who calls in response to your classified ad concerning the property.

5. Know the rules about signage and use multiple signs or sign groupings.

6. Get your real estate Web site up and running (see the next chapter).

7. Blanket the neighborhood with flyers about your house.

8. If you cannot sell your house quickly with all of these methods, try an auction.

Pitfalls Recap

TOO LAZY TO PACK UP AT THE END OF THE DAY? IT'LL COST YOU! Don't allow yourself or your contractors to get lazy and leave tools laying around the job site. It will invite petty thieves to break into your property and it will slow down the entire rehab process.

KNOW THE RULES ABOUT SIGNS. Be sure to find out about any restrictions the neighborhood may have regarding the use of multiple signs in the yard.

DOING REAL ESTATE ONLINE

OH, WHAT A TANGLED WEB WE SHOULD WEAVE

THE INTERNET has become a vital tool for any serious real estate investor. If you are going to get into this business and make a profit, you must have a Web presence. It's too easy to create and maintain a good Web site to pass up the opportunity. You'll get too much benefit from it not to incorporate the Web as part of the marketing for your company.

There are many good hosting companies around, and some of them work specifically with real estate investors (see the Resources section). Web design firms that work specifically with real estate investors have a lot of features and benefits to offer that would not apply to other types of businesses or Web sites. At the time of this writing, the cost of establishing a site is a onetime set-up fee of $24.95 and a monthly hosting fee of $24.95.

The very first day my site was published was a Friday. As on most Friday afternoons I had new classified ads coming out. I had not included the Web site address in the ads because I had no idea it would be up and running so fast (technology is amazing). When new ads come out in the paper, the number of incoming phone calls always picks up considerably. The first time the phone rang after the Web site was up and running I ran to get it. I was hurrying because I wanted to be the first person to tell someone, anyone, that we had a Web site. I had written our Web address (www.Barnett.Property Fast.net) in bold letters and placed it next to the phone. Sure enough, the phone call was from a real live prospect.

Yolanda was her name, and she had read the ad about our newly rehabilitated home. Yolanda said she wanted to see the house. This was just what I was waiting for. I told her, "You can see the house on our *new* Web site. That way you'll have a good idea if you're interested before you drive all the way out there." I was glad Yolanda was a prospective buyer because whoever called first was going to hear about the Web site whether they needed to or not.

About an hour later Yolanda called and said she was on her way to the property. She asked if I could meet her there to show it.

PITFALL: THE NEED TO SHOW THE HOUSE
There are a few things you *need* to be in charge of and showing houses is not one of them. You will spend way too much of your valuable time traveling to a property only to be left standing outside the house like a security guard on the graveyard shift. People will let you drive to the property and not think about calling you to say they aren't coming. There is a way to avoid this kind

of hassle. Go to a home improvement store and pick up a lockbox for about forty dollars. It will be some of the best money you will ever spend on your business. A lockbox holds the front door key. This way, anyone with the code can get the key, enter, and leave without your being there.

I was able to say that I would not meet her at the property because the house had a lockbox on it. All I did was ask her these two important questions: "If I give you the code to the lockbox on the house, will you promise me you'll lock it back up when you leave? And will you call me when you've left the house to tell me it's locked up again?" These two questions will get prospective homebuyers to make a commitment to you. Yolanda readily agreed. She was about to see her new home for the very first time, and she didn't even know it.

About an hour and a half later my e-mail chimed, alerting me that there was an unread e-mail in my mailbox. As I opened the e-mail, I was shocked to see Yolanda's credit application. It's one of the standard forms you can select to be on your Web site from the INET inventory of forms and reports. She loved the house and wanted to move forward immediately. I forwarded the credit application over to one of my mortgage brokers for a quick review. A few minutes later he called saying, "It looks OK, not great." It was my decision if I wanted to provide Yolanda with seller financing or reject her application. I was just as excited as she was, but it was important not to let my enthusiasm cause me to make a bad decision.

I called Yolanda back to go over some basic interview questions I use for all prospective buyers. These questions include: Are you going to pay your mortgage on time? Do you promise you're going to pay your mortgage on time? Do you swear you're going to pay your mortgage on time? How much money do you have for the down payment on your new home? I was looking for a minimum $7,000 down payment. Yolanda only had $5,000. What do we do now? Remember, this is your business, so you can do whatever you think is a good business decision. I asked Yolanda if she could do anything else to come up with the other $2,000. She offered a creative solution, one I was quite happy with. Yolanda proposed an additional payment of $500 per month for the next four months until the needed down payment had been reached. I agreed.

Yolanda had her first house, and I had sold a nice piece of my inventory.

That's how I sold my first house on the Internet, but that's not the last one. What I am about to share with you is the most exciting thing to happen in our industry since I have been involved in it.

eBay

Yep, little old eBay. At the time of this writing eBay is selling a house every five minutes. There are over 10,000 homes for sale in theUnited States on eBay right now. Most realtors do not understand that they are dinosaurs living in the ice age. They are one step away from being extinct, and most of them don't even know it's cold outside. Before you dismiss this comment, ask any travel agent if the Internet impacted their ability to make a living. The travel industry was revolutionized by the Internet, and it will be the Internet that revolutionizes the real estate industry.

According to its Web site, eBay is already the second largest seller of property in the United States. You already know you can sell just about anything on eBay; now you can sell houses as well.

Let me walk you through my first eBay auction of a house and then I'll catch you up on the latest. Mark Dove, a mentor of mine, showed me how to launch an Internet auction on eBay.

The Object: To Build You a Buyer's List

A very important part of any Internet business is the database you build. Any Internet trainer worth his or her salt will tell you, "The money is in the list, the power is in the list." The "list" is actually a database of customers and potential customers. By using a database builder, you can capture the e-mail addresses of the bidders on your auctions.

Before you jump to the conclusion that I am spamming people, please note that when a person bids at one of my auctions, they automatically receive a "pop-up box" asking them to confirm, "YES, I would like to receive information on additional properties in this area and price range that carry the same seller finance options as this auction." I am getting near 100 percent positive response from bidders to the pop-up box, which creates an "opt-in" list of buyers. These buyers are looking for a home in a specific area of town in a specific price range.

Don't panic if you don't know what a pop-up box is. If you go to www.AreYouDUMBEnoughToBeRICH.com and hit the menu button titled "MYAUC," I'll show you an exciting piece of Web ware. MYAUC (My Auction Company) is the system I personally use to create and control my auctions.

The system puts my auctions on autopilot and tracks all the information necessary for accounting and building the buyer list.

Why is building a buyer list so important? Imagine this: You're out looking at property to buy. You have concentrated your buying on a few subdivisions in what the industry refers to as "bread-and-butter" houses.

As mentioned elsewhere in the book, bread-and-butter houses are homes built in the last twenty-five years with three bedrooms, two baths, a two-car garage, and somewhere between 1,200 to 1,700 square feet. These houses are in moderately priced subdivisions. As an example, the medium-price house for the Dallas/Fort Worth market at the time of this writing is anywhere from $80,000 to $130,000 depending on its location.

You are in this particular subdivision because over the last few weeks you have built a buyers list. Your buyers list probably contains more than one hundred names of potential buyers. You know how much of a down payment each buyer is working with. You also know the highest monthly payment a buyer can afford. Armed with this information you make a startling discovery.

**It is easier to find homes for buyers
than it is to find buyers for homes.**

This is one of the secrets of building a million-dollar-plus business in a short period of time. To build this size business you must be thinking outside of the box. You must do things that others believe will not work, and you must have your systems in place to put as much of your business on autopilot as possible. The building of a buyers list is one such endeavor.

As you are driving through a subdivision, you are able to see deals you would have missed without your buyers list. The number-one expense in creative real estate is holding cost, and the buyers list cuts this down to a minimum.

Holding cost has for years been one of the major reasons investors leave the business. Holding cost eats away at your profit until there is nothing left, and then comes the blood, your blood, in the form of cash.

The buyers list allows you to sell properties in the shortest amount of time, thereby cutting your holding cost down to a bare minimum.

I was selling a HUD property I had recently finished rehabbing. The traffic on the property was brisk. The house was a basic bread-and-butter home; in fact, it was a little on the small side. But because it was in the right price range and in the right neighborhood, I was getting a lot of potential buyers. I accepted a full-price cash offer. Mind you, the price was considered over market by the few real estate agents who viewed the property, but I was able to get it in cash. Almost immediately after I accepted the cash offer, another couple saw the property and fell in love with it.

PITFALL: I ALREADY HAVE A CONTRACT, THANKS FOR CALLING

Many new investors will let potential buyers slip through their hands because the home they are selling is off the market and they do not currently have another home in that area. Please do not allow this to happen to you. When someone calls you concerning a property for sale, be sure to get several pieces of information from them:

1. Their complete contact information, including e-mail address.

2. How much of a down payment are they working with?

3. What is the biggest monthly payment they can currently afford?

4. Is this the only area of town they would consider living in?

5. What are the bed and bath requirements for their new home?

6. How soon will they want to move into their new home?

This is the information you will need to build a solid buyers list.

The young couple was looking to move into this particular school district. The house I had just accepted the full-price cash offer on was just what they were looking for. I suggested they allow me a couple of weeks to find a suitable property for them.

I went back to the HUD list because I knew there were more properties available in this school district. Since I had a buyer already lined up, I bid more aggressively than I normally would have. Within a week, I had purchased another home very similar to the one they had seen. Before I started any work on the house, I had the young couple come out to see what might be their new home. They loved it. We wrote up the contract and I closed with HUD as fast as possible. After the closing I started the rehabilitation process knowing the house was sold.

Of course some glitch with my name on it was waiting out there. Approximately ten days into the rehab, which meant we were a few days from completion, I got a call from the husband. He was close to tears as he told me he had been fired that morning. He called me before he called his wife. I assured him there would be no problem with letting him out of the contract, and of course his earnest money deposit would be promptly refunded.

This could have put me in a poor position because I had paid a little more for this property than I should have. Now I have to sell it again, and if it takes very long all of my profit will be eaten up with holding costs. Lucky for me I have a buyers list. I simply went back to my buyers list and started calling everyone on it who had said they were looking for a home in that area. After several calls, an older couple said they were hoping the contract on the original house (the house from the beginning of the story) would fall through so they could buy it. I told them the original contract was going to close but I had purchased another home in the area. They eagerly came to look at the new house, which was near completion. They loved it and made a full-price cash offer. That's why it is so important to build a buyers list.

Internet Auctions Help Build Buyer Lists

Internet auctions are the fastest way to build your buyer list. As we walk through the first of my home auctions, you will see how quickly the buyers list builds.

The aforementioned Internet whiz Mark Dove showed me how to build an auction on eBay using the MYAUC Web ware. Pay close attention here, because I do *not* auction houses on eBay. *I auction the down payment and provide seller financing for the remainder.*

You now know how to provide seller financing on all of your properties as covered in the last chapter. Having the ability to provide seller financing on any of your properties gives you a distinct advantage over the traditional real estate market.

When you post an auction on eBay using the MYAUC Web ware, you first post the auction's headline. Next, put the statement, "You are bidding for the DOWN PAYMENT on this house—The seller is offering seller financing." Later in the body of the auction (where we have the description and pictures of the house), add the statement, "The seller has the right to approve the winning bidder's credit." This last statement allows you to retain complete control of the auction. Since you are providing a mortgage for the winning bidder, you must retain the right *not* to sell to that bidder based on their credit.

To see my first auction and what my auctions still look like, go to www.AreYouDUMBEnoughToBeRICH.com and click on the menu button titled, "My 1st House Auction." Be sure to notice the counter at the bottom of the auction. It shows there were over 1,200 potential buyers visiting this property online. All of this occurred in the span of ten days. If we had over 1,200 people walk through a house in ten days, we would probably have to replace the carpet.

There were twenty-three bids placed on the house and twelve new additions to my buyers list. But the real power comes from the six e-mails I received from interested parties who did not bid. These potential buyers came straight to me. One of them was a man from Oklahoma who needed to move to the area quickly. He ran a distributorship and had the opportunity to take over the much larger Fort Worth territory. His credit was perfect, and he had $30,000 available for a down payment. He did, however, have one very specific concern. Since his distributorship operated off his personal line of credit, he wanted to be sure the mortgage I was carrying for him did *not* show up on his credit report. Are you kidding me? Not only can I make sure it doesn't show up, it is no problem at all. You see, we have to go through the time and effort to report it to the credit agencies; it does not happen automatically.

Remember the phrase, "The seller has the right to approve the winning bidder's credit." Because the phrase was part of the auction, I was now able to go back to the winning bidder, whose online bid was $5,000 and give them the opportunity to match the $30,000 down payment offered outside the auction. The winning bidder had poor credit, but I wanted to be sure to give them the opportunity to match the $30,000. If they had been able to match the down payment, I would have sold them the house even though their credit was worse than the gentleman from Oklahoma. The winning bidders were unable to even come close to $30,000, so it was my prerogative not to approve their credit. Because of this type of circumstance I will always pester you to stay in control of your business. Learning that one phrase is worth way more than the cost of this book.

Education is expensive; ignorance is costly.

Chapter Summary

1. Go to www.AreYouDUMBEnoughToBeRICH.com to sign up for your personal real estate Web site. Click on the menu button titled "Own Your Own Web site." Remember it's $24.95 to set up, with a $24.95 monthly hosting fee.

2. Go to www.Barnett.PropertyFast.net to see what a functioning real estate Web site looks like. It may not be the grandest site on the Web but it certainly gets the job done.

3. Go to www.AreYouDUMBEnoughToBeRICH.com to review the MYAUC Web ware. Click on the menu button titled "MYAUC."

4. Go to www.AreYouDUMBEnoughToBeRICH.com and click on the menu button titled "My 1st House Auction" to see what a functioning eBay real estate auction looks like.

Pitfalls Recap

DON'T BE CHEAP. It is going to cost you to build your million-dollar-plus business. It is called, "the cost of doing business." Spend a little and earn a lot.

THE NEED TO SHOW THE HOUSE. The cheapest employee you will ever have is a lockbox. Do not let buyers waste your time with property showings.

eBAY AND REAL ESTATE. Learn how to hold auctions on eBay for the down payments on your properties.

I ALREADY HAVE A CONTRACT, THANKS FOR CALLING. Don't fail to build a buyers list. Remember: It is easier to find homes for buyers than it is to find buyers for homes.

ALTERNATIVE
REAL ESTATE

THERE ARE things you can do to make money off real estate without having to actually take possession of a house or even buy it for that matter.

In this chapter is a system to earn $500 to $4,000 in the next 30 to 45 days. Some of you may be thinking, "I didn't buy this book to earn an extra $500 per month. I already know how to say 'Would you like fries with your order?'" Yes, but do not underestimate this system because it can easily grow into a $100,000-plus per year addition to your real estate income. I have found there are so many different ways to make money in real estate that it makes sense for us to examine them all and follow the areas that resonate with us personally.

So how do we put cash in your pocket in the next 30 to 40 days?

Private Mortgages

This country has a surprising number of privately held mortgages. Private mortgages are mortgages that have been created by an individual and not a traditional mortgage source like a bank or mortgage company. This is an extremely simple part of our business. There are only a few questions you need to be able to answer to get you started in the buying and selling of private mortgages. They are:

- How do we find these private mortgages?

- How do we make contact with the owners?

- What do we say to the owners once we make contact with them? What you say when you make contact with private mortgage holders determines your success. Later in this chapter I will give you another simple, yet powerful script anyone can use to get started.

- After we have used the script and someone has said "yes," what paperwork do we need?

- What do we do with this "yes" once we have it?

- And the most important question of all, how do we get paid?

- One remaining question concerns the people who say "no" to our offer: Do these prospects still have any value to us and if so what?

This chapter will provide the answers to these questions.

Location, Location, Location

Location is the number-one concern with real estate. And so it is with private mortgages. I am going to give you two methods of finding privately held mortgages. You will be tempted to go directly to the easier method first. Don't give in to temptation. It will short-circuit your ability to find the correct information that you will need.

First go to the Land Records Office at the county courthouse. It may be called a different name in your county, but anyone at the courthouse should be able to direct you to the correct office. Once you are in the Land Records Office, ask the clerk, "Where can I view the mortgages held for the county?" In public records, privately issued mortgages are not separated from those issued by public institutions (i.e., banks or mortgage companies).

Please remember, all mortgages must be filed with the county or they cannot be enforced. In other words, when a mortgage is filed with the court, the county recognizes the debt and will allow the mortgage holder to foreclose on the property if the payments are not made in a timely fashion. So for that reason anyone who has issued a private mortgage will have it filed with the county for their own protection. As soon as it is filed with the county, it becomes a matter of public record. As a citizen of the United States you have the right to review all public records during normal business hours.

So now you know where to go to find these privately held mortgages. Once you have located the proper office, you will find there are several ways counties have these records stored. If you live in a very small county, you may find the mortgages are still filed on paper and you will have to look through the actual documents for the information you need. You may find the county is a little more progressive and has stored these records on microfiche. This system is much better but is still a far cry from counties where the records have been stored on computer. This is currently the most common form of storage around the country. There is even a small number of counties (somewhere around 8 percent) that have put records on the Internet. Every day new counties are coming online with more and more of their public records, so your work will increasingly become easier.

While looking at these records, you want to look for the issuer or holder of the mortgage. Most often you will see the biggest names in the mortgage industry: like Countrywide, Household Finance, GMAC Mortgage, Chase, and Bank of America. Occasionally you will see a private name like John Q. Public.

John Q. Public sold a piece of property a few years ago and decided to hold the mortgage himself to make it easier to sell. After finding a buyer Mr. Public was happy with, he wrote a purchase and sale agreement between himself and the buyer. To accompany the purchase and sale agreement he created a real estate lien note, or mortgage. The mortgage details the amount of the total purchase, the down payment, the total amount financed by the mortgage, the interest rate, what the payments are, and what happens if the buyer defaults on the note. This mortgage was then filed at the courthouse to make it enforceable. This is exactly the kind of person you are looking for.

Now that you have located a privately held mortgage, you need several basic pieces of information including the name of the mortgage provider, the address of the property listed in the mortgage, the amount of the total purchase, the down payment, the total amount financed by the mortgage, the interest rate, and the amount of the payments.

Most of these mortgages will be first mortgages, but there are also benefits from finding a second mortgage. With second mortgages you must be aware that they are normally much smaller than the first and are sold at a much deeper discount. This means less money for you.

Once you have collected twenty to twenty-five of these names, leave the courthouse. You've probably put in a full day anyway, but even if you didn't you should leave. Leaving helps you shift gears to the next step.

Now you have names but not phone numbers. You have several options here:

1. The white pages of the phone book

2. Directory Assistance if you're lazy like me

3. The Internet at sites like: http://www.anywho.com; http://switchboard.com; http://simDetective.net

Before you start calling these people you need to prepare what you're going to say.

The Keys to the Kingdom Are the Words

The words for the script hold the keys to the kingdom. And like most things that are highly successful, the script is very simple. Here's what you should say when you call these private mortgage holders:

> "Hi, my name's _____. I was at the courthouse today and noticed that you provided a private mortgage on the property located at [give the street address of the property here]. My partner and I buy private mortgages for all cash and I was just wondering if you'd like to sell yours for all cash?"

There are only three answers you are likely to get: *Yes, No,* or *Maybe, how much are you willing to pay?* Two of the three answers are positive. Are you going to get some *no's?* Of course, and are you going to get some people saying, "That's none of your business, how did find that out, how did you get my phone number?" Of course. As I've said before about what my Dad taught me: "All they can do is say no. They can't shoot you and eat you." It puts things in proper perspective doesn't it?

Let's get the no's out of the way first. If someone tells you they are not interested simply reply with, "May I leave my name and phone number with you should your circumstances change in the future?" A reasonable, straightforward and simple request. You'll want to retain the information gathered on the people who say no and stay in touch with them. One way to stay in touch is to contact them every few months with a postcard. People's needs change, and the need for cash is usually one of the quickest things to change.

Now for the good stuff. What are we going to do with the ones who say *yes* or *maybe?* Let's go back to our script and pick up with the conversation with our prospect.

"Great, let me confirm the information I saw at the courthouse."

Now do exactly that. After you have reconfirmed the information you gathered at the courthouse, tell your prospect, "Let me talk to my partner about this and I'll get back to you in the next forty-eight hours with an offer. Is that fair enough?" And get off the phone. The more you say at this point, the less likely it is you are going to buy this private mortgage. Besides there really is nothing more to say at this point.

The next step is to get in touch with private mortgage buyers to see what they would be willing to offer you for the mortgage. For the sake of this book, I am going to talk about a generic mortgage buyer I'll call CASH Funders USA.

Who's Writing Our Checks?

For a list of current private mortgage buyers go to www.AreYou DUMBEnoughToBeRICH.com and click on the menu button marked "Private Mortgage Buyers." The companies listed are very active in the purchase of privately held mortgages.

All through the script you have been using the word partner. I know many of you are thinking, "I don't have a partner." You do have a partner; you just aren't aware of it yet. Your partner is the funding source or the private mortgage buyer. And this partner is the best type of partner, a partner for this one transaction. If you want to do business with him or her in the future, great, but that's up to you, and it should be a case-by-case decision.

Once you have a private mortgage holder showing some interest in selling his or her mortgage, even if it is only to find out what it is worth, you have something to go to a mortgage buyer with. A quick call to CASH Funders USA reveals there is interest on their part in buying this mortgage from John Q. Public *through you.* It is at this point I should probably tell you something very important.

Take a deep breath. This is where most new investors around the country start to squirm with lots of questions going around in their heads. Questions like, "What's to keep CASH Funders USA from going directly to the seller, leaving me out of the deal? How do I know CASH Funders USA is going to pay me?" And my favorite, "If this is all there is to it, why doesn't CASH Funders USA just hire a room full of telemarketers and deal directly with all of the John Q. Public's out there?"

These are all fair questions and let me answer them. First, "What's to keep CASH Funders USA from going directly to the seller and leaving me out of the deal?" Well, to be quite candid, nothing. Oh my, that wasn't what you were expecting to hear, was it? And the real answer is nothing except good business sense. I am sure there are companies out there who might do that very thing. That is why it is important to go with companies with excellent reputations like the ones I've listed on the Web site. But the truth of the matter is this: It just doesn't make sense for these companies to try to beat you out of one lousy check for a few grand. Please take a minute to look at this from their prospective, and it will answer all three of the questions at one time.

From a business standpoint, CASH Funders USA could probably cut you out of a deal very easily. You, being irate about this, would probably immediately file suit against them. This would result in both of you quickly spending more than the commission on the deal in attorneys' fees. And as in almost every suit filed in America, there is only one winner—the attorneys. Chances are CASH Funders USA will not take this route.

CASH Funders USA could just go out and hire telemarketers to do the work you've done, but they won't do that either. There are several reasons for this. First, they have to actually have a telemarketing room for these employees to work in. That typically means a long-term commercial lease for office space. Next, they've got to furnish the space because we can't expect these skilled people they're about to hire to work sitting on the floor. So a furniture lease is created for desks, tables, and chairs. There has to be a coffee break room because they have to take care of their employees. Then comes the fun part: They get to go through the wonderful experience of interviewing around 300 applicants to fill just fifty telemarketing spots. Once they hire people, they get to provide them a benefits package. To be competitive, they have to include vacation days, sick days, family leave, and the all-important health insurance. This all has to be in place before the first call is made. They can do all of this, or they can just pay you a nice commission to bring in all the private mortgage sellers you can find.

Make $500 to $4,000 in the Next 30 to 45 Days

Let's say that CASH Funders USA has received the information we gathered from the seller and now has an offer to buy ready for us. They contact us and say they are willing to pay $85,000 for John Q. Public's private mortgage, which currently has a balance of $100,000. We now must call John Q. back and tell him, "My partner and I would be willing to pay you $82,000." Let the private mortgage holder respond before you make another sound. In fact, I don't even want you to breathe until the private mortgage holder responds to the offer.

Our money suddenly came into the picture. If the private mortgage holder says yes to our offer, we call CASH Funders USA back and they then draw up the purchase and sale agreement. CASH Funders USA sends us the contract and we get it signed by the seller. Once the contract is signed, we deliver it to CASH Funders USA and they take over from then on. We are notified of the closing date and go by the closing office to pick up our check. It's just that simple. Please note, CASH Funders USA closes with the private mortgage seller for the $82,000, and we are paid separately. This prevents the private mortgage seller from seeing our fee.

Chapter Summary

There are other ways to make money in real estate without buying and selling houses. One such way is to find a buyer for privately owned mortgages and take a commission. This will not be enough to be your sole income, but it can certainly supplement your real estate career. Look into alternate investments and try working with private mortgages.

Pitfalls Recap

Not acting on this chapter's information.

BECOMING A LIEN, LIEN, LIENING MACHINE!

AS I MENTIONED before, I never put my own money into real estate deals. That practice started out of necessity and stayed with me because it makes more business sense.

Let me explain my thought process here. I can provide a service to investors who are looking for a better return than they would get in the stock market. As you may know, a few *trillion* dollars left the stock market between 2000 and 2003. Much of that money is looking for a new home and much of that money is just gone. If I can provide an investor with an investment that will earn approximately 10 to 12 percent and that certainly has less risk than stocks, then I can have all the money I want to do real estate deals with. I will not be limited by my personal net worth or credit. When I can then invest my personal funds in state-administered investments yielding 20 percent or more, isn't that what I (and you) should be doing? You bet.

For example, Florida has an 18 percent flat fee the first year on liens purchased "over the counter." Over the counter means the liens were not sold at public auction. Iowa offers 2 percent per month— that's *24 percent per annum.* Are these rates even legal? Yes, these are legal interest rates, and they are set by the state governments. Perhaps that sounds too good to be true, but its not. I invest my real estate profits in tax liens.

Some of you are cringing when you heard the word "taxes." I don't like paying taxes any more than the next person, but taxes can be opportunities. You can make money and save money from taxes with either tax liens or tax credits or both. (Tax credits are covered in Chapter 19.)

There is a thriving industry selling tax liens and certificates from delinquent property taxes, and you should take advantage of this kind of investing.

In certain states, when a property owner is late paying property taxes, the state and/or the county will issue a tax lien on the property. (Though most taxes are covered in mortgage payments, there are many, many properties around the country—a lot more than you might imagine—for which taxes are paid separately from the mortgage.) Think about it: If a property owner doesn't pay property taxes on time, the county or municipality will still need money to provide the public services we all enjoy. But now they're short on cash. You know what you and I call that, right? Too much month left at the end of the money. So to raise cash, they sell tax liens or certificates. That is, when property owners become delinquent in paying their property taxes, the state and/or the county sells liens or certificates for what the property owners owe. That's right—I can buy liens or certificates that give me the right to collect not only back taxes, but also interest, steep interest, on what they owe. When we buy these liens or certificates, we are buying the right to receive the taxes on the property. We are also buying:

1. The right to receive the interest owed on the taxes.

2. The right to foreclose on the property should the taxes not get paid (referred to as the redemption period ending).

3. The right to obtain the title of the property through foreclosure should the redemption period end.

4. The right to evict the residents (only after we have foreclosed and only if we have to).

5. And the right to dispose of the property as we wish.

These are very attractive benefits, so as you might imagine, these lien sales are getting more and more popular. Most people are unaware these opportunities even exist.

Buying Liens

In states where tax liens and/or certificates are sold, there is a specific process for selling the liens and certificates. There is a specific process for selling tax lien deeds and a specific process for a tax lien foreclosure. All of these processes are regulated by individual state laws. You will have to check with the state in which you're going to be buying liens for details. But here's how the process generally works:

1. A property owner becomes delinquent in his or her property taxes.

2. If the property owner does not pay, the taxing unit, county, or municipality holds a public auction. The taxing authority then sells this "accounts receivable" (the amount owed) to investors as liens or certificates. The amount owed may include back taxes, interest, penalties, and legal, administrative, and/or court costs.

PITFALL: IT'S PASSED DIRECTLY TO YOU

Do not get caught up in what is included in the lien price. In fact, it doesn't matter whether it includes lawyer's fees, penalties, etc., since these will be passed directly to the taxpayer. The one thing you have to watch out for is that the lien is not more expensive than the property itself, but usually this is pretty easy to tell.

Please note: When you buy a lien, you are not buying the property. You are buying the right to receive what the taxpayer owes the state and/or the county for their property. However, and this is the best part, if the property owner doesn't pay you the amount owed, the property becomes yours through the foreclosure process, and you can now sell the house. What a cheap way to obtain property.

PITFALL: BUYING LIENS FOR
THE WRONG REASON

Many investors around the country focus on the fact that they could end up with the property when they are buying liens. What they and you should be focusing on is the terrific rates of return made on tax liens. If you get the property, think of it as winning the lottery. It will be great if I win, but I'm not going to lose any sleep over it if I don't.

Back to the auctions: Auctions begin with a minimum or opening bid for the amount of property taxes the property owner owes. In some cases this may be as low as a few hundred dollars, and it can easily go to $30,000, $40,000, $50,000, and more. Even if it is as much as several thousand dollars, if the property goes into foreclosure, you just bought an incredibly cheap house. Why would a homeowner risk losing his or her house for such little money? Only God knows for sure, but they do. And this can be an incredibly lucrative part of your real estate portfolio because of the interest you receive. And every now and then, someone wins the lottery.

Remember: Not every state is a *tax lien* state. Some states are called *tax deed,* some are called *tax certificate* or *auction states.* In some states, the minimum opening bid is either for the market value of the house or for the total amount of the judgments against the property. Needless to say, these kinds of investments are not as lucrative as tax liens. Don't fall into deal fever and buy a bad investment just because you can. Focus on investing in the tax lien states—it will get you richer faster. Go to http://www.AreYouDUMBEnoughToBe RICH.com for "The 7 Golden States of Tax Lien Investing."

In most states, the county collects the money from the property owner and then pays you. I prefer to invest in these states because the county does all the work—collection and payment. The county is, of course, enforcing the state law, so they are more likely to get paid than a private investor.

How Liens Make You Money Fast

All you have to do is purchase a lien at a state or county auction or tax sale. You start earning money *from the day you buy it.* The property owner not only owes you the amount of the lien or certificate— they owe you interest starting from the sale date. This interest is considered *legal interest.* This means that the interest rate is set by the state law and must be paid. There are no exceptions. The interest rate can only be changed by an act of legislation—and we know how long and difficult it is to change legislation. This interest adds up quickly, so the homeowner will either have to pay up quickly, pay you huge interest rates, or relinquish the property. When it is paid in full, the homeowner can redeem the certificate. In some states the homeowner pays you directly; in most, however, the funds go through the county. Either way, you make loads of cash or the property is yours.

To give you an idea of how profitable this actually could be, consider the case of billionaire Wayne Huizinga reported in *The Miami Herald*. He was the founder of Blockbuster Video and obviously a very smart and rich guy. Unfortunately for him, he owed a little over $47,000 on one of his million-dollar properties. It turns out it was just a mix-up by people working for Mr. Huizinga, which resulted in the taxes not being paid. The property was sold for back taxes and some smart investor got a million-dollar property for a little over $47,000.

PITFALL: LOOK AND LEARN
BEFORE YOU LEAP

Not every lien is a windfall. Spend the time learning the bidding system in the state *before* buying. It is possible, though not likely, that the property may not be worth the amount of the lien. Again, it is not important what the state includes in determining the opening bid so long as the bid is less than the value of the property. You want to make sure that, if you foreclose, you can get back substantially more than what you paid for the lien.

Now, if you're like many Americans who invested their hard-earned money in the stock market only to lose it, you understand how truly valuable liens are. Owning a tax lien not only guarantees you a fixed interest rate by law; you may also gain a property. In fact, the worse the economy is doing, the better the tax lien deals are. When times are bad and unemployment is high, the number of tax liens, and therefore the number of deals, goes up significantly. What's more, tax liens are one of the best guaranteed interest-earning investments you can make. These rates don't change unless legislation changes. With tax liens, you are earning interest on your investment *virtually risk-free.*

Of course, there's risk in everything, but if you do your homework, you can very rapidly grow your real estate profits. Here's what I suggest you do:

1. Determine which state you want to bid in.

2. Find out when their tax sales are.

3. Learn the bidding process.

4. Learn how to give proper notice for foreclosure (if necessary).

5. Determine whether the lien is a deal (whether the price is less than the value of the property).

6. Make a bid.

It's that simple. Remember: We are in a simple business. Not an easy business, but a simple one. Overthink this and you will miss out on some incredible investment opportunities.

OK, There Are Some Risks

Who wouldn't want to get in on a deal where they either get a great interest rate or a home extremely cheap? OK, slow down a little. As with any investment, there are some risks.

The first risk is to get so caught up in making a deal that you buy something you can't afford.

PITFALL: DO YOU HAVE THE DOUGH?

I know I've mentioned this one before, but it bears repeating. Before you make an investment, make sure you have enough money to cover all the costs involved. If the homeowner fails to pay and you foreclose on the property, do you have enough to pay attorney's fees and taxes until you resell the property? Don't forget to include the time it would take to evict the homeowners. Similarly, don't make a bid you can't pay for. It would really be embarrassing to get sued by the county.

This is serious, folks. Make sure you have more than enough money to cover all possible costs, or the "investment" will end up taking money out of your pocket rather than putting money into it.

Another common risk is just not knowing enough about the laws in the state you are buying the liens in.

As I mentioned before, you should never buy a property without first inspecting it. This also holds for liens. Never buy a lien without doing actual inspections and geographical surveys. If you don't, you run the risk of paying too much for a deed. One way to do this is to build relationships with real estate agents in the area where you want to buy. They can help considerably when you are trying to find out whether the property is a good deal or not. For example, maybe an area shouldn't be built on because it gets flooded periodically. Wouldn't you want to know before you bought it? Local realtors can help with this kind of information.

Which Are the Best States to Invest In?

Texas, Florida, Arizona, Michigan, and Iowa are excellent states in which to invest in liens. Texas offers a 25 percent penalty. Florida offers 18 percent interest, and Iowa has a 2 percent per month interest rate. To give you an idea of how this adds up, an investor can earn 48 percent in two years in Iowa. Where else can you get such incredible money? Again, check out the Web site to see which states offer other great deals.

In most states, you don't have to live in the state or physically be at the public auction to buy a lien. You could buy liens either by mail or online. Just make sure you're diligent about doing the research.

Take a Vacation

If you're not fortunate enough to live in one of the better-paying states (e.g., Texas or Florida), take a vacation to check out the area. It's the best way to check out specific properties and do research. It will also make a trip tax deductible. (As if you need an excuse to take a vacation.) Many nice vacation spots like Florida and Hawaii also sell liens. Just make sure you actually do some work and keep good records.

This Is Where I Put My Money

As I mentioned in the beginning of this chapter and elsewhere, this is the kind of investment I make. I want to have high interest rates *guaranteed*. What's better than 20-plus percent rates legally guaranteed? I'll tell you what's better...those kinds of rates, legally guaranteed, and backed by real estate. If the owner doesn't pay, I get the property for the incredibly low price of the lien.

Now you understand why I don't put my money into real estate deals. *I take my money out of real estate and buy liens.*

Chapter Summary

If you want to be a millionaire, you have to start acting like a millionaire. Don't accept anemic interest rates or risky stocks. Seek out the better investment, do the research, and start making some real money.

In the next chapter, we will discuss the best-kept tax secret in America.

Pitfalls Recap

IT'S PASSED DIRECTLY TO YOU. It doesn't matter whether it includes lawyer fees, penalties, etc., since these will be passed directly to the taxpayer.

BUYING LIENS FOR THE WRONG REASON. What you should be focusing in on is the terrific rates of return made on tax liens. If you get the property, think of it as winning the lottery.

LOOK AND LEARN BEFORE YOU LEAP. Not every lien is a windfall. Spend the time learning the bidding system in the state *before* buying. It is possible, though not likely, the property may not be worth the amount of the lien.

DO YOU HAVE THE DOUGH? Don't make a bid if you can't pay for it. It would really be embarrassing to get sued by the county.

IF DEATH AND
TAXES ARE CERTAIN,
LET'S BE DEAD CERTAIN
ABOUT TAXES

Fire Your CPA!

IF YOUR CPA is not a real estate investor, fire this person. Your CPA is a team member who is too important not to be great. It is my opinion, humble though it may be, that if your CPA is not a real estate investor, this person can't possibly know all of the rules affecting your tax return.

The best way to find an excellent CPA is to interview a few. In Chapter 21, I'll go into depth about building a dream team and tell you how I go about finding each member. As far as CPAs go, you need to interview them carefully. All you have to do is call them on the phone, or better yet, go by their office for a short face-to-face.

PITFALL: THE BIG EIGHT, I MEAN THE BIG SIX, OH WHO CARES, STAY AWAY

In the last couple of years the integrity of the large accounting firms has pretty much been destroyed. I was never in favor of using these firms anyway. If you are a small business, do you want your taxes prepared by a recent college graduate who's been made a junior partner or do you want them done by a grizzled veteran who's been around the block a time or two? Maybe you could even find a grizzled veteran who actually owns investment real estate himself and is not struggling to move out of his first apartment.

PITFALL: BUT I DO MY OWN TAXES, I EVEN HAVE SOFTWARE

One the biggest pitfalls you can fall into as a real estate investor is doing your own taxes. Regardless of the fact that you are an extremely intelligent person (you bought this book, didn't you?), some things are just better left to the professionals. If you own a copy of tax accounting software, also known as the IRS's Best Friend, you may be even more dangerous than you thought. Do yourself a favor and throw it in the pool; it will probably serve you better. It's time to take the proverbial financial revolver away from your temple and don't walk, *run* to a competent CPA. All you want to make sure of is that you have the best CPA possible. Let the pros do what they do best.

Before I leave the CPA issue I want to invite you to go to the Web site http://www.AreYouDUMBEnoughToBeRICH.com to receive a free gift. At the site please click on the menu button marked "Free Tax Review." CPA Roger Kerbow will take a look at your current situation for free and make his recommendations. Of course he is a real estate investor—I only work with people who specialize in real estate.

Do I Hold for Long Term or Sell for Quick Cash?

And the answer is…yes. Yes, you should hold for long term, and yes, you should sell for quick cash, but it's up to you to decide when to do what. Here's what you need to consider: What are your needs? We all want to build long-term wealth, but does the investment take care of your immediate cash needs? It is my suggestion to take care of all of your cash needs first and then worry about building long-term wealth. Here is one good way to answer the fast cash or long-term hold question: let your CPA review your personal situation and be your guide. Maybe you'll receive a call like the one I got from my CPA a couple of years ago saying, "You have to stop selling everything you get your hands on. You're sending more money to Uncle Sam than you have to. Start keeping some property." A call like this will certainly make it easier for you to make the transition from selling everything to starting to hold some property.

One of my CPA's favorite sayings is, "Nobody depreciates me anymore." Of course he's talking about real estate when he says it. Your CPA is one of your business partners. Just because he may not have any ownership in your business does not mean he is not a business partner. You are selling your CPA short if you do not consult him on a regular basis about your business. A good CPA can help make sure you are getting all of the benefits you are entitled to on a property. The amount you can depreciate on your taxes can become quite large when you have multiple properties.

Long-Term Capital Gains

A good CPA can sit down with you and quickly show you the beauty of long-term capital gains. At the time of this writing, long-term capital gains are running right at 18 percent. When your business is just getting started and the money hasn't started flowing in yet, this may not seem like a big deal. But as your income starts to go up dramatically, you will see why they are so wonderful. Long-term capital gains, depending on your tax bracket, can mean as much as a 20 percent or more difference in the amount of taxes you have to pay. This is money straight out of, or into, HIP National Bank. If you want to make money in real estate, you have to realize that this business is about getting good at creating deposits. To create extra deposits from long-term capital gains, all you have to do is hold a property for one year and one day.

When you are selling property, you can sell it using a lease-purchase option. The lease-purchase option allows you to retain the actual ownership of the property while you have a buyer already in place. By putting your buyer into the property using the lease-purchase option, you can easily retain ownership of the property for the required one year and one day, thereby qualifying you for long-term capital gains while keeping the buyer around. After you have had your lease-purchase buyer in the property for a year, you can convert the lease-purchase to a straight purchase. If the buyer has made their payments on time, you should be able to get them qualified with a mortgage-only loan.

Taking Advantage of Your IRA

This seems like the perfect place to shift gears and get into another tax-related area your old CPA might not have made you aware of. I say your old CPA because many of you should have realized by now that you are using the wrong CPA. Let me put the disclaimer right here:

**I am not a CPA. I am not qualified
to give you personal tax advice.**

I am, however, a taxpayer. I am a taxpayer who uses a great CPA, and I can give you ideas to talk over with your own qualified CPA.

Did your old CPA discuss with you the facts concerning your IRA account? Did your CPA discuss your ability to own property inside your IRA account? I didn't think so. If you want to make your IRA account have explosive growth over the next few years, start putting real estate inside your IRA.

PITFALL: THIS MUST BE SELF-DIRECTED

To be able to hold real estate inside your IRA account, your account must be self-directed. Self-directed means you have the ability to decide which investment option your money is invested in. Make sure your account is self-directed before trying this.

Like many of you, I had no idea I could have real estate inside my self-directed IRA account. I spent almost ten years in the financial services industry, and during all of those years I had some type of involvement with retirement accounts. And yet, I didn't know. So if your broker is unaware of this investment option, don't be surprised.

PITFALL: BUT MY BROKER SAID
IT COULDN'T BE DONE

You may have just called your brokerage firm and been told that you can't put real estate inside your IRA. And the brokerage firm is correct. You can't put real estate inside your IRA account with *them.* There are only a few custodial companies across the United States capable of holding real estate inside your IRA.

It is the custodial company's decision as to which investments they will allow inside the accounts they are the custodian for. All custodial firms *must* work within the IRS guidelines of what is acceptable for an IRA investment, but within the IRS framework companies can decide what they will and will not mess with. Most just do not want to deal with anything they think is as complicated as real estate.

PITFALL: WATCH WHO YOU TAKE ADVICE FROM

A while back I blasted a stock broker who was pestering me to get some business, any business, from me. He finally got to the point of practically begging me to just transfer my IRA to his firm. He wanted to build a broad-based stock portfolio with representation in several different industrial sectors. He advised, "It's dangerous to keep all of your wealth tied up in real estate. What happens when the real estate market turns soft?" To his question I responded, "My wife and I will be partying in the streets. When the real estate market turns soft, it is the traditional real estate market turning soft. And when the traditional real estate market turns soft, our market, the non-traditional real estate market, goes from good to *great*." Then I stopped his calls from ever coming in again when I asked him, "Have you ever considered why they call you brokers? Maybe it's because you're *broker* than the people you're trying to advise." Somehow he failed to see the humor in my statement, but there is a valuable piece of advice contained in the statement and it is this: be very careful who you take advice from. Don't allow yourself to listen to people who tell you things can't be done just because they can't do them.

> Don't allow yourself to be guided financially by people
> who would have to take out a bank loan to take you to
> McDonald's. Listen to people who are doing what you
> want to do and are doing it very successfully. Find peo-
> ple who are making a multiple of your income and want
> to help you. This thought process has guided me faith-
> fully for the last seven plus years, and I heartily suggest
> you give it a try.

Once you find a company that specializes in self-directed accounts in which you can hold real estate, like Mid Ohio Securities*, all you have to do is to transfer some of your existing self-directed funds to that company. They will help you get the account open, and then you're going to start having some fun. It is a lot of fun to see your IRA account start to grow exponentially because you are doing a few real estate deals per year in it.

Here's my suggestion: Let one of your financial goals be that you are going to do one real estate deal in your self-directed IRA per quarter. One per quarter is enough to make your IRA explode. Be careful how many deals you do per year; more than five or six and your IRA account could be considered a business in itself. If that happens, you'll lose all of the tax benefits the IRA provides. Let the folks at the custodial company worry about the details. You should concentrate on finding the deals.

Won't I be exceeding my yearly contribution amount if I am buying real estate inside my IRA? This is a question I hear almost every weekend when I'm teaching. Please do not confuse your $3,000 yearly IRA deductible contribution amount with the performance of an investment inside your IRA. Any time you buy real estate for your IRA,

---

* There are only four companies that do real estate, and this is the only one with which I have personal experience. These companies are not easily found.

it should be with little or no money. According to several real estate attorneys I have spoken to across the country, it only takes $100 to make a real estate contract binding. Follow me here. This is important. If I transfer some uninvested cash into my self-directed IRA account and I find a great deal on a piece of real estate that I am buying with no money down, I can have the custodial company make the purchase inside my IRA. For example, if I have an account with Mid Ohio and I find a great property to buy with no money down, I could have Mid Ohio cut a check from my self-directed account to the seller of the property. The check will be from Mid Ohio Securities For The Benefit Of The Bill Barnett IRA, Account number XXX-YYY-ZZZ. In all of the contracts, the "buyer" will be Mid Ohio Securities For The Benefit Of The Bill Barnett IRA, Account number XXX-YYY- ZZZ. If you do this, you will then own a piece of real estate inside your IRA. The next step is to sell the property and create a deposit. Only this time the deposit you are creating will be for your IRA. In my example above, after I have successfully marketed the property, all of the proceeds will be made out in the name of— you guessed it—Mid Ohio Securities For The Benefit Of The Bill Barnett IRA, Account number XXX-YYY-ZZZ. *All* of the profits will go directly into your IRA. Let me repeat: *All* of the profit. You cannot take any of this profit out to spend. The proceeds must go completely back into the account. So if I do a deal for a hundred bucks and then sell it for a profit of, say, $20,000, you see how my IRA account will start to explode and how, if you do the same, you might actually be able to afford to retire somewhere down the road.

Long-Term Capital Gains vs. IRA Investing

Please note that the investment strategy for IRAs is exactly the opposite of that of long-term investments. There is a very important nuance you must be aware of when dealing with real estate inside your IRA account. Unlike long-term capital gains where you want to retain ownership of the property for at least one year and one day, inside your self-directed IRA account you *must* sell the property within one year, or your IRA account will be considered a business and you will lose *all* of the tax benefits.

To wrap up this very important chapter, I want to give you some powerful action steps to take and take NOW.

ACTION STEP 1: *Fire Your CPA!* Please don't lose the seriousness of this statement in my twisted sense of humor. Interview several CPAs until you find one who is a real estate investor. It can make a world of difference for you.

ACTION STEP 2: *Take the Time.* Go to my Web site and take advantage of the *free* tax review.

ACTION STEP 3: *Decide to Listen In.* While you are on the Web site, check out the *free* live weekly conference call. Decide you are going to be a part of the call for the next month. I promise you it will be informative and fun.

ACTION STEP 4: *Open Your Mid Ohio Self-Directed IRA Account with a custodial that will allow real estate investing.* It only takes a few minutes to complete the paperwork and transfer some cash to it. This small action step can set the ball in motion for you to build a truly significant retirement.

Chapter Summary

As you start making deals, it is extremely important to pay attention to tax legislation. If you don't, you may end up handing over your big bucks to Uncle Sam. By just holding on to your property for a little longer, you may significantly reduce the amount of taxes you owe by taking advantage of long-term gains. Similarly, you can take advantage of the fact that IRAs grow tax-deferred by investing IRA money in real estate. To do either of these things, you need professionals who specialize in real estate. Don't just take advice from anyone—real estate deals are too complicated to take a chance on uninformed amateurs. It pays to get a well-qualified CPA and a custodial company that specializes in real estate. Do your homework. For some leads on how to get started, see the resources section in Appendix B.

In the next chapter we will cover in more detail ways in which you can reduce the amount of yearly taxes you pay.

Pitfalls Recap

THE BIG EIGHT, I MEAN THE BIG SIX, OH WHO CARES, STAY AWAY. Hire an accountant who's a grizzled veteran and has been around the block a time or two.

BUT I DO MY OWN TAXES, I EVEN HAVE SOFTWARE. Don't do your own taxes. Regardless of the fact that you are an extremely intelligent person, some things are just better left to the professionals. Make sure you have the best CPA possible and let the pros do what they do best.

THIS MUST BE SELF-DIRECTED. To be able to hold real estate inside your IRA account, your account must be self-directed. Self-directed means you have the ability to decide which investment option your money is invested in.

BUT MY BROKER SAID IT COULDN'T BE DONE. There are only a few custodial companies across the United States capable of holding real estate inside your IRA. Make sure you work with them.

WATCH WHO YOU TAKE ADVICE FROM. Don't allow yourself to listen to people who tell you things can't be done just because *they* can't do them. Listen to people who are doing what you want to do and are doing it very successfully. Find people who are making a multiple of your income and want to help you.

TAX CREDITS

THE BEST-KEPT SECRET
IN AMERICA TODAY

ONE OF THE greatest training tools for budding young real estate investors is the board game Monopoly. If, like me, you played Monopoly when you were growing up, there were probably certain things about the game you liked best. One of the things I liked best about the game was Monopoly money—the ability to start the game with a wad of cash and start purchasing real estate all around the board. It just doesn't get any better than that. Then as we grow a little older, reality sets in. Most of us forgot about real estate and focused on real money-making opportunities, like getting a *job*. You remember your job. How did Mark Victor Hansen describe a job? Oh yeah, Just Over Broke.

But a few of us luckily found our way back to real estate. We can now look back at an entertaining children's board game and realize what a terrific introduction to real estate it was.

A much smaller number of us found out a shocking truth as adults. Monopoly money really does exist. Only today I call it the best-kept tax secret in America.

Tax Credits

Before you jump to any conclusions about what you might think tax credits are, read a few more pages and then decide.

So what are tax credits? Specifically what are affordable housing tax credits? Affordable housing tax credits are not about low-income housing. There are low-income housing credits but I'm not really interested or involved in those. I am very interested and involved in affordable housing *tax credits*.

Let's start with what they are and why they exist. Affordable housing tax credits are designed to provide affordable housing for the exploding market segment of older Americans. You know who I'm talking about. When we were under thirty, we called these people senior citizens or the elderly. When we hit our forties, they simply became older. And as life progresses, we realize just how young these people really are. These people, people just like you and me, these aging baby boomers make up the largest segment of our population. Finding affordable housing for this segment of the population is a major concern.

One of the ways the federal government has found to encourage investment in affordable housing is with the use of tax credits.

WHY TAX CREDITS?

Why are tax credits such a strong inducement for investors? Because, in my opinion, there is no better way to cut your taxes than through tax credits. It's true that deductions reduce your amount of taxable income, *but credits cut your actual tax bill, dollar-for-dollar.* That's right, a dollar-for-dollar reduction in your taxes. That's because credits come into play *after* your tax liability is figured. For example, if your CPA figures out that you owe the IRS $1,000, and you have a $1,000 in tax credits (also known as IRS Monopoly money) you can pay the taxes with the tax credit dollars, *in full.*

BUYING TAX CREDITS

How much money is available every year in tax credit dollars? At the time of this writing, $33,000,000,000. I wrote the number out so you could see what thirty-three billion dollars looks like. In other words, there are plenty of tax credit dollars to go around. You may be wondering: With that kind of money lying around, how come not everyone is taking advantage of tax credits? That's a good question. Why weren't you doing it before now? I'll bet it's simply that you weren't aware this opportunity even existed or that it was available to regular folks just like you and me.

HOW MUCH AND HOW LONG?

One reason this opportunity is available for any of us is the cost of getting your tax credit account started. Please note, I will only advise you of the companies I know of on a first-hand basis. There may be additional companies out there offering the same type of services, but I only use the ones I believe to be the best. In the case of tax credits, the best is a company called Boston Capital. Opening your Boston Capital Tax Credit account will require a one-time investment of $5,000. If you wish to make additional tax credit purchases later, they can be made for as little as $2,000 per purchase.

Once you have purchased your tax credits, please be aware that you should retain the investment for its full term, which is ten years.

SELLING YOUR UNUSED CREDITS

Another well-kept secret is that you can sell your unused credit. If you are eligible for a tax credit but don't take the full amount, you can sell the remainder. Similarly, if you need a tax credit, you can buy one from someone else. About 90 percent of tax credits are bought by corporations like Warren Buffet's Berkshire Hathaway, American Express, Exxon, Home Depot, Merrill Lynch, CBS, Microsoft, and banks. (Yes, banks buy them too. One of the banks I do business with bought a *million dollars* worth of tax credits.) The remaining 10 percent is required by law to be reserved for individual investors.

I hope this is enough information to get you to a competent CPA, one who's versed in tax credits. I could write an entire book on tax credits. Hmmm, there's an idea.

LOW-INCOME HOUSING CREDIT

Another housing credit you should be aware of is the low-income housing credit. The low-income housing credit can only be claimed for residential rental buildings in low-income housing projects that meet specific requirements.

Also, the homeowner's property tax credit program helps low-income homeowners by limiting the amount of tax they must pay on their property. Generally, the property's tax bill cannot be more than a fixed percentage of the homeowner's income. In effect, the law limits what the homeowner can be charged.

REHABILITATION TAX CREDIT

Whenever you've done any work on a house, check with your CPA to see whether you are eligible for the rehabilitation tax credit. Needless to say, you should keep impeccable records of what you spend on what. Technically, the rehabilitation credit applies to costs you incur for rehabilitation and reconstruction of buildings on your property. Why would the IRS allow this? It provides incentives for investors to bring money into the low- and moderate-housing market. Rehabilitation may include renovation, restoration, and reconstruction. It does not include making the building larger or adding a new building to the property.

Generally, the percentage of costs you can take as a credit is:

- 10 percent for buildings built before 1936
- 20 percent for certified historic structures

The IRS has special briefs for things like facade easement, property leased to a tax-exempt entity, use of the rehabilitation tax credit by lessees, and differences between the historic rehabilitation tax credit and low-income housing tax credit. In fact, if you go to their Web site at http://irs.gov, you can do a search for real estate tax tips to get a general idea of what you might qualify for. I don't recommend that you try to weed through these on your own—it just helps to get a sense of what is out there. Let your CPA do it. That's his job.

BUT WAIT, THERE'S EVEN MORE!

Now I'm no tax expert, so I can't give you tax advice. You'll need to talk to your CPA for that. (Hopefully you took my advice in Chapter 18 and found a qualified one.) However, I know that there are two types of tax credits, and one is more valuable than the other. There are refundable credits and nonrefundable credits.

Refundable credits may eliminate any tax you owe and provide you with a refund. That means that even if you don't owe anything, you could get money back from the IRS by claiming the credit. These credits include:

- Earned income tax credit
- Additional child tax credit

◆ Credit for taxes withheld on wages and other amounts

Nonrefundable credits can reduce what you owe to nothing, but you can't get money back from the government. Nonrefundable credits are:

◆ Child tax credit

◆ Child and dependent care credit

◆ Credit for the elderly or disabled

◆ Adoption expenses credit

◆ HOPE and Lifetime Learning education credits

Now here's the part many people don't realize: Although nonrefundable credits can't be used to get a refund on your tax return *this year,* the unused amount can be carried over from year to year until the credit is absorbed (or the carry-forward period expires, whichever is first).

STATE TAX CREDIT PROGRAMS

Every state also has its own tax credits, and you should have your CPA review them with you to make sure you are taking everything you can. There are some tax credits that are particularly important for real estate investors to know about, and as I've already said three of those are the affordable housing tax credit, low-income housing credit, and the rehabilitation tax credit.

Real estate may simply be the best legal tax shelter available. The IRS offers you, as a property owner, specific and valuable benefits. For example, you can:

◆ Indefinitely put off paying taxes on your real estate investments. This is known as deferring your tax liability. If you time things right, you can control when you pay your taxes on capital gains. If you followed my advice from Chapter 18 and got yourself a good real estate CPA, she should be able to help you do this.

◆ Deduct many real estate expenses such as property taxes, utilities, interest payments, insurance, legal fees, and ordinary maintenance fees.

◆ Claim depreciation of your property, which allows you to increase your deductions and lower what you currently owe.

◆ Exempt the profits from selling a primary residence for up to $500,000 for a married couple. That's right, Congress passed a law in 1997 that exempted profits from selling your own home (Remember: It has to be a primary residence) up to $500,000. Obviously there are restrictions, but I'll let your CPA tell you about them.

Of course, this was just a taste of the tax benefits you can get from being a real estate owner. I wanted to whet your appetite a little (taxes can be so dull and painful).

Additional Benefits
DEPRECIATION
While the above-mentioned expenses are generally considered deductible, any costs that are associated with building or improving your property cannot be deducted. If an improvement adds permanent value to the building or property, it is considered a capital expenditure and cannot be deducted. For example, a septic system or new roof would be a capital expenditure. The costs of such a purchase would be averaged out over the life of the expenditure. You can then deduct the expense gradually.

Residential real estate and improvements can be depreciated over twenty-seven-and-a-half years. If the property is not residential, you can depreciate it over thirty-one-and-a-half years.

DEDUCTIONS

Deductions are another powerful way you can reduce your taxes. Make sure you deduct everything you are entitled to. As a real estate investor, some of these things may include:

- Property taxes—whatever you pay your local government.

- Insurance—premiums for things like fire or mortgage insurance may be deductible. Check with your CPA.

- Interest—whatever interest you pay on your mortgage. This money really adds up.

- Utilities—for your rentals.

- Miscellaneous operating expenses—for your real estate business or rental properties. These expenses may include things like repairs, mowing the lawn, gardening, upkeep, legal fees, telephone, or supplies.

Again, the key to making sure you get all your deductions is to keep very good records and to get a good CPA who knows the industry. Some things you may think are deductible expenses are actually considered capital expenditures. This means they can't be deducted, but they can be depreciated.

Some Terms Defined

You're probably dizzy from all the terms, so I'm going to slow down and explain some of them that are important to us as real estate investors.

Capital gain is the term for the income (or profit) you receive from selling a property. This income is not treated as ordinary income (like a salary) and is taxed at a different rate. There are limits to what you can deduct as capital gains in any given year. However, your CPA can help you to either carry over some of the capital gains to subsequent years or reinvest the money.

Depreciation is taking the cost of a capital expenditure and averaging it out over the expected life of the improvement. For example, if you bought a new floor covering that you expect will last ten years, you divide the cost of the floor by ten. This is the amount you can deduct each year for the next ten years. (This kind of deduction can affect your capital gain, as is explained later in this chapter.)

Tax deferral is reporting earnings, but legally delaying payment of taxes by using a long-term payment plan. This can lower your taxes by postponing payment to a year when you think your taxable income will be less than it is today. Gains from investing money in real estate can be deferred indefinitely.

Now that you have an idea of what some of these things mean, back to the exciting part. If you don't know what some of these following items mean, you should because they can save you a lot of money in taxes.

Beware of Restrictions

Be aware that there are some restrictions. (Aren't there always?) Passive activity rules may apply and may prevent you from taking the credit. Generally, a passive activity is any rental activity or any business in which the taxpayer does not "materially" participate. Nonpassive activities are businesses in which the taxpayer works on a "regular, continuous, and substantial basis." So before you can figure out whether you can take the credit, you have to determine what kind of income you are earning.

Types of Income and Losses

Here is a little more clarification. The IRS divides your income into two categories:

> *Passive:* This includes rentals and businesses without material participation. (For example, a limited partner is generally passive because of more restrictive tests for material participation. As a result, limited partners will generally have passive income or losses from the partnership)

> *Nonpassive:* Businesses in which the taxpayer materially participates. Nonpassive income also includes salaries, any kind of guaranteed payments, 1099 commission income, and portfolio or investment income. (Portfolio income includes interest income, dividends, royalties, gains and losses on stocks, pensions, lottery winnings, and any other property held for investment.)

PASSIVE ACTIVITIES

There are a number of activities that the IRS deems passive. Real estate investors should be aware that these activities are generally considered passive:

- ◆ Equipment leasing

- ◆ Rental real estate (with some exceptions)

NONPASSIVE ACTIVITIES

In contrast, income and losses from the following activities are generally nonpassive:

- ◆ Salaries, wages, and 1099 commission income

- ◆ Guaranteed payments

- ◆ Interest and dividends

- ◆ Stocks and bonds

- ◆ Sale of undeveloped land or other investment property

- ◆ Royalties derived in the ordinary course of business

- ◆ Sole proprietorship or farm in which the taxpayer materially participates

- ◆ Trusts in which the fiduciary materially participates

Confused? That's why a CPA who specializes in real estate is so important. Do not underestimate the need and worth of a good accountant.

ONE GIANT PITFALL

The more you depreciate, the higher your taxable income when you sell the property. Depreciation can help lower your current taxes, but unless you reinvest in another property or another tax shelter, you may ultimately increase your taxes inadvertently.

To avoid this and other pitfalls, you have to make sure you know what you're doing. (Enter experienced real estate CPA.) You also need to regularly reevaluate your investments and the potential tax consequences of what you are doing.

Chapter Summary

There are numerous advantages to being a property owner. Make sure you make use of them. This chapter should have given you at least a sense of what is out there. You should get a qualified CPA, one who owns investment real estate himself, to speak with you and review your situation. Just remember, there is no reason you should pay more taxes than you are obligated to pay, so buy some tax credits, use your deductions, and depreciate if necessary. This will help you keep your hard-earned money and put you on the way to making millions. My personal CPA, Roger Kerbow, reminds me constantly, "Bill, it's not how much you make, its how much you *keep!*"

In the next chapter, we will review the three stages of being a millionaire.

Pitfalls Recap

ONE GIANT PITFALL. The more you depreciate, the higher your taxable income when you sell the property. Unless you reinvest in another property or another tax shelter, you may ultimately increase your taxes. Make sure you go over this with your CPA and decide what's right for you.

HOLY COW, YOU'RE
A MILLIONAIRE!

AS YOU START your real estate investing career, you'll go through many discoveries and changes, both professionally and personally. There will also be some landmarks or stages you'll pass though. Some of these changes are the three stages of being a millionaire. It is a very important to recognize these three different stages as you pass through them because of the effect they will have on who you are.

The first of these stages I call the *Asset Millionaire*. The asset stage of being a millionaire marks the first watermark of your career. It is the easiest stage to reach, and it may also be the most important. As you start purchasing property, I want you to keep track of the market value of the property. You need to do this so you will know when you are controlling a million dollars worth of property.

How do I track this asset stage? It is a simple process of keeping a record on paper of each property as you buy it. For this calculation I do not care if there is an outstanding mortgage on the property or not. We will deal with outstanding liens later. All that is important in this stage is the market value of the property. Once you are controlling a million dollars worth of property, you will be an Asset Millionaire. Once you realize you are a millionaire in this very simple and basic way, it will make it much easier mentally for you to move through the other two stages. For so many people the millionaire status is such a far-off goal or dream that it may seem unreachable. Once you become an Asset Millionaire, you will have proved to yourself that you can be a millionaire. Going forward, all we are going to do is apply a different definition to the term. Make no mistake about it—your banker is not going to shake your hand the next time you're in the lobby and congratulate you on reaching this milestone. It may have little or no impact on your lifestyle, but what it can do for your self-image can be huge. As children we learned to walk before we could run, and becoming an Asset Millionaire is our equivalent to walking before you run. And in the real estate investing world, *running is fun!*

Congratulations! For some of you reading this book on the West Coast, namely in Los Angeles, San Francisco, or San Diego, and on the East Coast, in maybe the most exciting city on earth, New York City, you'll blow through this stage very quickly. There are several other areas of the country where the average prices for homes are very high. Those of you living in these areas are ahead of the game. You must realize it works to your benefit to have higher pricing for an average home. *It certainly does not work against you.* Ron LeGrand says it very simply: "The more money you play in, the more money sticks to you."

I couldn't have said it any better myself. I have a friend in New York City whose very first deal was more than a million dollars.

When we decided how much money we wanted to make, we used the formula for the average price of a house as our basis to see how many deals we needed to do. We are now going to use the same formula to track our progress to being in control of a million dollars worth of property. This initial accumulation of property will build our confidence if we recognize it for what it is. It is a necessary step to reaching the second stage of becoming a millionaire.

The second stage of becoming a millionaire is what I call an *Equity Millionaire*. Now we are now going to shift gears and apply a new definition to the word "millionaire." In the "equity stage" of becoming a millionaire, we will start to see a dramatic impact on our financial statement and net worth. The equity stage is tracked by now keeping up with all the outstanding liens we have on any of our properties. If you are used to evaluating your net worth, this is a very similar process.

When we evaluate our personal net worth, we take the value of all of our assets and deduct all of our debts from it. The result of this equation is our net worth. In the equity stage of becoming a millionaire, we are going to take the value of all of our investment property and deduct all of the outstanding liens from that value. The result of this equation is our equity. This is the number we use to calculate our progress in becoming an equity millionaire. As we accumulate more and more property, this goal will become easier to reach. Now we *are* starting to have an impact on our net worth. As we gain more and more equity in our properties, our lifestyle may start to change and change very quickly. As we gain more and more equity, remembering of course that our equity and the profit derived from each property will be very close to being the same number, some of the properties in our portfolio will start to sell. As these properties start to move off your books and into your bank account, you will be exchanging equity for cash. You will be creating deposits.

PITFALL: THE CART BEFORE THE HORSE

Take care of first things first. Many investors get started in our business and want to start building up their long-term portfolio of keeper properties. They want to create a new stream of steady cash flow by keeping property and getting a small monthly check. After they've done a few deals, they find their lifestyle hasn't changed at all, and they look at all the work they have put into their career. They have nothing to show for it but a few hundred dollars a month in spread. This can be very frustrating.

The Dumb Enough investor, however, gets into this business and sells properties for the big check first. By getting the big checks first, you can eliminate your daily cash needs. Once these daily needs are out of the way and you have a solid cash reserve, *then* you can start to build your long-term wealth. But you have to keep *the cart before the horse.*

PITFALL: LET'S NOT GO CRAZY

It's right here that so many investors lose what little common sense they brought to the party to begin with. As these big checks start to come in, it can be very easy to go "toy crazy." Toy crazy is when we get our hands on large lump sums of cash and immediately run out and spend it. This spending is most commonly used for toys. Believe me, I know what I'm talking about here. Nobody loves a good toy more than I do. And you

> *deserve* lots of great toys. All I am asking you to do is
> to put toys in their proper place: second. Toys are sec-
> ond to being smart with your money. After you sell a
> property, please put 20 percent—yes, 20 percent—of
> the profits back into the company account. By doing
> this, you'll always have enough money to do little things
> for your business. Little things like marketing. Do not cut
> off the head of the goose that lays the golden eggs,
> which is exactly what you'll be doing if you spend it all.

Now you have purchased enough property to have your equity exceed a million dollars. Congratulations, you have become an Equity Millionaire.

Let's get into some serious fun and some serious business with the third and final stage of becoming a millionaire. This final stage is what I call being a *Fun Millionaire*. It is, of course, the most challenging and the most rewarding of the three stages.

As a Fun Millionaire you are able to put your hands on one million dollars in cash within seventy-two hours—if it's an emergency. What do I mean by that statement? First, let's cover the seventy-two-hour part of the statement. For you to be able to put your hands on a million dollars in cash within seventy-two hours, you *cannot* have this money invested in real estate, right? Real estate is not liquid enough for us to be able to convert it to cash within seventy-two hours; we just can't sell real estate that fast. This means we will have to have this money invested in other areas—areas like money market accounts, CDs, and other short-term, highly liquid investments.

This may seem like a far, far away goal as you read this, but it will come quicker with real estate investing than with any other investment vehicle I know of. There is light at the end of your investing tunnel and it's *not* a train. It is your future and it's a bright one.

As this "sudden" wealth starts to come to you, it will become more and more necessary to look at things like asset protection and tax credits. Please talk to a good financial planner with a well-rounded base of knowledge. The best way to find these advisors is by asking people, especially people with money. Let them know your financial picture is changing and you would like some solid advice, and ask if could they recommend anyone. Make sure you have at least one years' worth of lifestyle dollars set aside, just in case.

Take advantage of the educational IRA accounts available to provide the cost of a college education for your children and grandchildren. Remember that you can do three to five deals a year inside your retirement account without having the IRS consider your IRA account a business. After you had made the investments for your personal account you can open an account for your kids or grandkids and contribute to them. Know when you are doing this that you are planning for your future and for future generations of your family.

With money comes *responsibility*. Does that sound as if I just took all the fun out of the entire book? You have enough responsibility in your life, and I'm trying to give you more. As it says in the Bible, "Every one to whom much is given, of him will much be required." There are several things you can do to properly handle your money. As you reread the book—you are going to reread the book, aren't you? Good! As you reread the book, have three highlighters handy, a yellow one, a green one, and a pink one. Go back through the book and highlight the areas pertaining to the management of your money with the green highlighter. Use the pink highlighter to mark items that are "action items" or "hot items." These are things you need to do now. Many of the marketing suggestions will need to be marked as "hot" or "action." The yellow highlighter is used to mark areas dealing with nontraditional thinking. You want to highlight those areas with the yellow highlighter because they require caution. These are areas that are normally criticized by friends and relatives. My suggestion is for you to be careful and use caution when you discuss what you are starting to do with you free time—relatives and friends may try to dissuade you.

PITFALL: DON'T LET ANYONE RAIN ON YOUR PARADE

It is a very common practice in our world today for people to say, "It can't be done." Many times these words of doom and gloom come from seemingly well-meaning friends and family who appear to thrive on the negativity created when they get to squash your dreams and goals. Until you have a few deals under your belt, keep what you are trying to accomplish to yourself. Please tell everyone you can about your desire to buy real estate, but if they are not selling you any real estate themselves, *how* you buy real estate is none of their business.

As you start to implement these strategies and build your business and your financial freedom, please think about good debt versus bad debt when you are spending your profits. Good debt and bad debt are in a constant battle for your money. Picture them as the two small spirits of good and bad sitting on your shoulders and constantly whispering in your ears, always trying to influence you. The Bad Debt Devil will be telling you to spend all of your proceeds when you sell a house and create a deposit. The Bad Debt Devil will tell you things like, "Wow, I didn't know it would be this easy. It's OK to blow this entire amount. You'll be doing deals so fast you'll never even miss this one check." This type of thinking from the Bad Debt Devil will create more problems than it solves. The Good Debt Angel will remind you to pay yourself first, to keep 20 percent of every sale in the business account. The Good Debt Angel will remind you how making money can also be very rewarding in a nonmonetary sense because you are helping investors get an excellent rate of return and putting people (like contractors) to work. The Bad Debt Devil may even get you to overspend when buying a property by straying from the formulas. The ultimate weapon the Bad Debt Devil has to work on you with is the stress he can create in your life. This stress is created when you don't manage your money properly. This can lead to a lot of stress in your home life. Financial stress is the number-one problem cited in divorce. If you love your spouse or significant other, it's simple: Do a few deals and relieve much of the financial stress that can creep into your life. Dear Abby couldn't give you any better advice herself.

Pitfalls Recap

THE CART BEFORE THE HORSE. Take care of first things first. Make a few big deals and increase your cash first before investing in rental properties.

LET'S NOT GO CRAZY. After you sell a property, please put 20 percent—yes, 20 percent—of the profits back into the company account. By doing this, you'll always have enough money to do little things for your business.

DON'T LET ANYONE RAIN ON YOUR PARADE. Don't let the negativity of others stop you from succeeding.

THERE IS NO I IN
THE (DREAM) TEAM

AS I'VE MENTIONED before, one of the biggest pitfalls when you first start out is trying to do everything yourself. Not only is this impossible, it will prevent you from earning your potential income. Your time should be reserved for making offers—offers that will bring in significant amounts of cash—not painting the walls or trying to figure out your taxes. A few well-chosen people will make your business run like a dream. They can help you get the most bang for your buck and free you to "concentrate on what is important and not what is urgent," as Stephen Covey says. So who do you need to make your business run like a dream? Who do you need on *your dream team?*

- *An attorney.* I know, I know, I'm not any more fond of attorneys than the next person, but I have several friends who are attorneys. My wife doesn't want me be seen with them publicly, but trust me—you'll need one.

- *Realtors, real estate agents, or brokers.* The National Association of Realtors is an organization of Realtors who work together. One benefit of working with a Realtor, real estate agent, or broker is that they have the Multiple Listing Service (MLS). This means that members within the network share information on properties they're representing. So if you list with one, you effectively list with all of them. But don't forget the lockbox technique described in Chapter 14.

If you do end up working with either an agent, broker or Realtor, make sure you:

- Develop a mutually beneficial relationship. Let them know what you can do for them, and do not waste their time.

- Let them know you'll be doing more and more deals and that you're looking for more than a one-shot relationship.

- Tell them exactly what you want from them. The more specific you are, the more likely it is that they'll be able to help.

- If they don't understand what you do, *do not try to educate them.*

I covered in more detail how to work with agents, brokers, and Realtors in Chapter 14. A few well-developed relationships can bring you several deals a year. Try to find people who specialize in such things as bank REOs or HUD foreclosures.

◆ *Appraisers.* Before you can get your tenant/buyer refinanced with a mortgage-only loan on the property, you'll have to get it appraised. Lenders want a qualified opinion of how much the property is worth based on an inspection and comps. They're trying to make sure their investment is not too risky. You, as a new real estate investor, should be equally thorough. You really need an appraiser for every property on which you're going to use the twelve-to-eighteen-month owner financing selling technique and on many of the properties you're thinking about buying.

When looking for an appraiser, of course you want to make sure he has a qualifying license. That's simply the difference between being DUMB Enough and being stupid. Your appraiser should be someone who understands the value of offering seller financing.

A good appraiser is worth her weight in gold. If you're about to sell a house or plunk down some private investor's money, you want to make sure you're both getting a deal. An appraiser is absolutely invaluable when we're selling a property.

◆ *Inspectors.* Equally as important as appraisers are inspectors. There are different kinds of inspectors, and you may want to hire more than one if you suspect there might be a problem with a house. There are, of course, licensed general home inspectors. But you also want to hire a structural inspector if you're looking to buy a property with foundation problems or if you're selling one with repaired foundation problems. For ethical reasons, you should not hire someone as an inspector who might be in a position to get money for fixing the problem. An inspector is vital in helping you to determine the Blood, Sweat, and Tears (BST) Value.

- *Pest-control inspectors.* There is nothing worse than watching a house devalue as it is consumed by carpenter ants or termites. Even evidence of such damage will reduce the value of your property. (And believe it or not, some buyers get turned off when they see a roach scurry by—picky, picky, picky.) Pest-control inspectors look specifically for damage from pests like termites, carpenter ants, beetles, and ants. Look for one who will give you a detailed written report of the damage along with diagrams of the property and a list of actions necessary to take care of infestations.

- When you are closing a deal—either by buying or selling a house—you will need *an objective third party* to take care of business during escrow. Escrow is the process of closing and completing all steps laid out in the contract. These include details like private or hard-money financing, inspection, payments (if any) to the seller, changing the title, and filing any necessary items at the courthouse. Depending on what state you're in, escrow will be taken care of by either a title company or an attorney. Find out which you need. If you're in a state that requires an attorney, make sure she he or she specializes in real estate.

When you are assembling your dream team, remember to bargain. If you mention that you're an investor and that you're likely to need their services on a regular basis, you can usually get a better price. Remember: You're not accepting anything less than a good deal.

Special Edition Dream Team for Rehabbers

In Chapter 7, I described a team of workers you'll need in order to get work done quickly. If repairs are needed, you want this team to be ready and waiting to work on the house as soon as you get the keys. The sooner you get the work done, the sooner you can start showing the house. As you should know by now, your profits start shrinking quickly if it takes too long to find a buyer, so you want the house in saleable condition ASAP.

For this special team, you should have:

- *HVAC (heating, ventilation, and air conditioning)* to inspect all of the heating and air conditioning systems. If it is an older home, you want to have the furnace or heat exchanger cleaned. You want to make sure the air conditioning has a full Freon charge and will put icicles on the end of your nose in July.

- *Plumbing* to make sure there are no major problems. The plumber is just checking everything out and making a list of recommended repairs. Most of these repairs will be performed by the handyman. You check the plumbing out yourself by looking for any water leaks or water damage. Make sure the toilets flush, the faucets don't leak, and the showerheads spray properly. (This is not an easy business, but it is a simple one.)

- *Painters* to make sure we can get on their schedule without having to wait for weeks. Aggressive painters can go ahead with most of their preparation at this time. This includes all of the caulking that needs to be done inside and out. You want the painting prepped so that when the painters return to finish their work, they can finish in a maximum of two days, one day for the outside and one day for the inside. I will tell you now: A good painting contractor is the hardest member of your trash dream team to find. When you start going to REIA (Real Estate Investors Association) meetings, you will notice a willingness of other investors to share their contractors with other members. Just ask about painting contractors, and you're likely to hear, "I don't know of any. If you find a good one, let me know." Of course they all use somebody, but if they are happy with them, you'll never get the name because this is the most difficult kind of contractor you can find. I freely share all of my contractors, except for my painters—they're that hard to find. Good luck and happy hunting.

◆ *Electricians* to make sure there are no major problems here. The main thing you want to check is whether the electrical panel is up to code. Additionally, your electrician can quickly look at all of the wall plugs and light switches to determine whether they're wired properly. The electrician can also determine whether any of the current wiring looks like a fire hazard.

◆ *Landscapers* are a problem area. I tried for over two years to work with several different landscapers. I was never able to locate one who understood I was a wholesale client. Finally, common sense prevailed and I simply had day laborers come in for landscaping. Your handyman should be a good source for finding workers who are available on a daily basis. This is an area where it is too easy to overspend. Keep it clean, neat, and colorful. Remember, it's all about curb appeal. What will this home look like to the prospective buyer driving through the neighborhood for the first time?

Locating Team Members

You want to find the cheapest, most qualified people available. Keep in mind that you don't need licensed contractors for every job. Only certain jobs—such as electricians—require such expertise. The rest of the time, you should try to use a qualified, nonlicensed person. Where do you find such people?

- Try your neighborhood home improvement store. Home Depot, for example, can be a goldmine. Ever wonder why employees seem to know how to use the products? Ever think about how those handy people giving how-to demonstrations learned how to do it in the first place? Home Depot hires professionals. Ask around. You may get lucky.

- REIA—The Real Estate Investor's Association, as I mentioned above, is a great place to locate these kinds of people. One of the benefits of belonging to an association like this is that you get to meet people in the same business who have similar needs. It's a great place to swap information.

- Classified ads. Don't overlook the obvious. Classified ads are a great way to find people who are looking for work. Just make sure you ask them enough questions to determine whether they are qualified.

- One of the best ways to find someone is through word of mouth. Ask everyone you know, especially those in the business. If you don't get tips on who to use, you will at least get advice on who not to use.

Evaluating Potential Team Members

When you're trying to build a team, think in terms of a team and not just contracting for specific jobs. You're looking for people who

- Will be available when you need them

- Will work quickly and accurately

- Are qualified, but not overpriced

- Will work well together

Although they are independent contractors, you hope they will do a good enough job that you will want to hire them again. You'll want to build relationships and work out the details early on. This should be a well-prepared team, ready to move in, get the job done, and get out. Also keep in mind that you will be providing them with work regularly, so you should use this as bargaining power when negotiating prices.

Though they will be working as contractors, they are in essence applying for a job. So when you are evaluating them, treat it like a job interview.

Let them sell you. Don't try to sell the job. Let them convince you that they are the best person for the job. Ask them questions like:

- How much experience do you have?

- Have you ever done this specific job before?

- Do you charge per job, per day, or per hour?

- How do you work best? Alone or in a team?

- Will you be able to work on this job while other work is being done in the house?

- How long does it take you to complete a job?

- Have you worked with these team members before? Do you think you can work well with them?

- Do you have insurance?

- Have any of your clients ever had a problem with your work?

- How did you deal with their complaints?

- Do you guarantee the quality of your work?

- What will you do if we decide we aren't satisfied with the quality of the work?

- How and when do you expect to get paid?

- Do you provide receipts? (You will if you expect me to pay you for it!)

- Are you permitted to work in this country?

When you are finished with the interview, ask for at least three references. And then check them! At least two references should be from satisfied clients. The last reference could be a character reference—someone who knows them well and can vouch for their character.

Developing Mutually Beneficial Relationships

If your team is only getting the job done and nothing else, you are not getting the most out of your team. To truly maximize your relationship, you should make sure your arrangement is mutually beneficial.

- Reward your team with cash for bringing you deals.

- Offer your contractors a bonus if they make the property especially sales-friendly. It's commonly known that you get what you reward. If you're trying to make your property easy to sell, reward your people for making it into the kind of place people will really want to buy. You'd be surprised what a little positive reinforcement can do to improve creativity and quality.

- Similarly, offer bonuses if the contractors finish early. Let them know that the sooner you can start showing the place, the sooner you can sell it. The sooner you sell it, the more money you make because you reduce holding costs. Pass some of these savings on in the form of bonuses, and you'll get results faster.

- When dealing with Realtors, agents, or brokers, offer to show them the rehabilitated property first if they were the one to bring you the original deal. You may get more Realtors working for you to find the deals in the first place.

The basic message here is:

> *You scratch my wallet, I'll scratch yours.*

Chapter Summary

Do yourself a favor and don't try to do everything yourself. You'll be doing yourself a great disfavor and you're just too valuable. Professionals will do a better job in less time and do it more cheaply. It pays to find a few well-qualified, not overpriced professionals to do this work. Not only will you get better results, you'll be available for making more deals.

The next chapter will review how to best use your dream team.

DUMB FOR 120 PUT ME ON THE ROAD TO PLENTY

PUTTING IT ALL TOGETHER

Your First Thirty Days: Setting Yourself Up for a Profitable Business

AS I MENTIONED in Chapter 3, Abraham Lincoln once said, "If I had eight hours to chop down a tree, I would spend seven hours sharpening my ax." These first thirty days are your "ax-sharpening" period. They are the most important thirty days of your real estate investing life. Many of you will worry if you haven't completed your first deal in the next thirty days. Stop worrying. What's most important is that you set yourself up in such a way that you can profitably spend the rest of your career. So concentrate more on getting yourself set up than on how soon you close your first deal. The first step is determining your goals.

Determine Your Real Estate Financial Goals

You'll get nowhere fast if you don't have set financial goals that will spur you to action. Everyone wants to make more money, but what does this mean in practical terms? On the first day of your real estate career, use this simple formula to figure out your financial goals:

> **The number of houses I need to sell** = **The amount of money I want to make / The average price of a home in the area**

Obviously you will need to determine the price of the average starter home in your area. Remember that our target house is a 3-bedroom, 2-bath, 2-car garage that is somewhere between 1,200 and 1,700 square feet, simply your basic 3/2/2.

You should also plan on having about thirty to thirty-five conversations to close one deal. To be on the safe side, let's push the number of callers to fifty. Out of fifty conversations with sellers you should be making at least ten written A, B, C offers. With ten written offers you should be closing at least one deal. Don't worry. As the weeks go by, your closing ration will increase.

> **Number of Conversations with Sellers per Day = 10 × 5 Days = 50**
> **Number of Written A, B, C Offers per Day = 2 × 5 Days = 10**
> **Number of Deals per WEEK = 1**

Now you can commit to your goals. Write them down.

> **I will make $_____ in the next 120 days through my real estate investments because I am DUMB Enough To Be RICH!**

> **I will need to sell** _____ **houses at an estimated $25,000 profit to make this goal.**
>
> **I will need to talk to** _____ **callers a day to reach my goal.**

Now you have your financial goals established and written down: the amount of money you want to make, divided by $25,000 equals the number of houses you have to sell in the next 120 days to make that happen; the number of sellers you need to talk to; and the number of written A, B, C offers you need to make in a week. Now that you know how many sellers you need to talk to, you can get started with your business.

GETTING CUSTOMERS

On days two through thirty you need to start getting sellers to call you and you need to find investors whose capital will enable you to make deals. One of your first objectives is to find that first house, that first deal which you will later sell for a profit. To get the deals, you need to get calling and you need motivated sellers to get to call you.

> **Use the Nine Surefire Ways to Get Motivated Sellers Calling You**
>
> **1.** Signs
>
> **2.** Classifieds
>
> **3.** Flyers
>
> **4.** Business cards
>
> **5.** New subdivision builders
>
> **6.** Direct mail
>
> **7.** Web site

8. Networking

9. Realtors, real estate agents, and brokers

There will be a short time period before these marketing tips will actually bring in some calls. While you are waiting, you may need to be more proactive about finding sellers and call some people yourself. You can, of course, go looking for sellers in traditional places like classified ads. Whether you find sellers or they find you, the process is the same.

When you are on the phone with a seller, you need to determine quickly whether or not it's a good deal. Don't get too excited and make a deal just because they are interested. You want to make sure the deal, especially the first deal, will be profitable and therefore a great deal for you. To figure this out, use the WOW script.

WOW SCRIPT

1. Worth: If you had the house appraised today, what would it appraise for?

How did you come up with that number?

2. Owe: What do you owe on the property?

Would you take what you owe for the property?

How much are your payments?

Are the payments P.I.T.I. (Principal, Interest, Taxes, and Insurance)?

Are the taxes and the insurance escrowed? If not, are they paid?

Are you paid up through the end of last month?

3. Want: What do you want, what are you trying to accomplish with this sale?

Are you telling me, if I don't pay you _____ for this property, then we can't do business?

OK, Mr./Ms. _____, let me put a pencil to these numbers and see if I can come up with something that will make sense for both of us. I'll give you a call tomorrow. Is this the best number to reach you at?

The WOW process is the same for every deal except for foreclosures and pre-foreclosures. When dealing with foreclosures and pre-foreclosures, you want to make sure you have more than enough money to get through the deal. Otherwise you may get yourself into hot water and be worse off than if you hadn't done the deal at all.

Once you find potentially profitable deals, you need to have the capital to make the deal. To that end, you need to start getting together an investment pool. Though you can certainly use standard financing companies, that really would be cutting into your profits. I prefer that you working with private investors. Use the following worksheet and script to start finding your own private investors. Try this on everyone whose name you know.

I know this is not for you, but who do you know that might be interested in earning 12 to 15 percent on their money, secured by a first lien on real estate for a short-term investment, six to twelve months?

Often I am asked whether it is a good idea to involve family and friends. There's some danger in this, especially with family. Essentially, you are darned if you do and darned if you don't. When I first started, I didn't ask my family because I thought they would feel pressured to invest and because I was a little more nervous making my initial deals. When my father found out I had been offering 15 percent on real estate investments and that I hadn't offered him the same thing, he was very angry. As I told my father, "I never had a deal go bad, but if I did, it would be with your money." Friends are a little better, because a friend may not feel as pressured to invest when you ask. Still, it is a very sensitive issue and you will have to make that decision yourself.

Days Thirty to Sixty: Expanding the Market You Deal With

After you have gotten the hang of buying and selling a couple of homes, you will want to expand your marketing a little. Of course you will stick to using the nine surefire ways listed above to bring in business, but here are a few other very profitable areas you should consider: HUD housing, foreclosures, and pre-foreclosures. Starting around day ten, you should begin looking at HUD houses, pre-foreclosures, and foreclosures. You may not be able to close a HUD deal quickly, but you can get acquainted with the brokers who specialize in this area and get into the habit of searching for the houses and viewing them regularly. Remember, focus less on how long it takes you to make a deal than on making the contacts and setting yourself up.

To review, here are the steps to buying a HUD home:

1. Locate the HUD inventory on the Internet by starting at http://www.hud.org.

2. Create a list of the properties you want to look at.

3. Find a HUD broker/agent.

4. Lay out your viewing route in the most efficient order to look at these houses so you can see the largest number possible in a single day.

5. Choose the properties you want to bid on.

6. Determine your price.

7. Make a bid.

When you determine a bid, you have to consider:

AS IS asking price   _____

BST number based on comps   _____

Minus contingency fee (10% of BST)   _____

Minus profit margin (20% of BST)   _____

Minus repairs (if needed)   _____

Equals the maximum bid of   _____

Maximum bid = HUD asking price $\times$ 82% _____

If the HUD number is greater than the maximum bid, then it should be good deal.

Once you buy a home, HUD or otherwise, you may want to make some improvements before selling out or becoming the mortgage company yourself. Here are a few ways you can control how much the property is worth.

Types of changes that increase property value:

◆ Physical improvements to property's exterior (e.g., landscaping, roofing)

- Physical improvements to property's interior (new kitchen, finished basement, etc.)

- Getting more money out of an income property by being the mortgage company (e.g. higher payments than rent would create)

- Converting a residential or vacant property to an income property

When making repairs, keep the following in mind:

- Use a handyman for most jobs

- Use a licensed contractor only when needed

- Heating and air conditioning (inspecting is a good idea)

- Electrical work (see if the electrical panel is up to code)

- Plumbing (make sure there are no major problems)

- Landscaping (use day laborers instead of contractors)

In addition, there are a few beautifying tips that you can take care of that really increase the value of the house:

- Resurfacing ceilings (certainly if there's been water damage)

- New light fixtures (e.g., ceiling fans for bedrooms, clear globe for other rooms)

- Improving walls (e.g., crown molding)

- Fixing/replacing doors (replace only when damaged)

- Flooring (e.g., carpet, vinyl for kitchen and bath)

FIVE STEPS TO BUYING A FORECLOSED HOME

When you are ready to expand into the pre-foreclosure and foreclosure market, use the five steps below to get you started:

Foreclosure Step 1: *Establish contacts.* Take a few hours in the next three days and call a total of at least five different banking institutions and finance companies in your area to find out who represents their foreclosed/REO property. Introduce yourself to these people. Get yourself on their fax distribution list. If they have a property you can close on within two weeks, tell the representative. Also put yourself in touch with real estate auction companies. Another great way to get contacts is by calling these five types of attorneys: divorce, probate, bankruptcy, real estate/title, and foreclosure.

Foreclosure Step 2: *Determine market value.* Establish the traditional market value of a property by using comparable sales (comps). Get your comps from Realtors, real estate agents, and brokers. Or you can become an associate member of one of the local boards of Realtors.

Foreclosure Step 3: *Have the cash ready for a quick close.*

Foreclosure Step 4: *Make the offer.* You will have to use the state-approved "purchase and sales" contract, which you can get from any title or escrow company. Go back to the Blood, Sweat and Tears (BST) formula found in Chapter 6, and make sure your offer is a win-win offer.

Foreclosure Step 5: *Create deposits.* Sell the property.

When dealing specifically with pre-foreclosures, the steps are a little different:

Step 1: Locate a pre-foreclosure listing service.

Step 2: Arrange for enough cash to cover the deal.

Step 3: Write and mail the pre-foreclosure letter to the list.

Step 4: Use the WOW method to weed out the bad deals

Step 5: Make the offer.

Step 6: Market the property and make some money.

While expanding your marketing, remember to keep track of the people who call you about a property. The easiest way to do this is through Excel. And you should start building this database as you start getting responses to the nine surefire ways to get motivated sellers calling you. Anyone who is interested in selling you a property is probably interested in buying something as well.

GET YOURSELF ONLINE AND BUILD A BUYERS LIST

Putting your business online both with a Web site and with eBay auctions is the fastest way to build your buyers list.

1. Go to http://www.AreYouDUMBEnoughToBeRICH.com to sign up for your personal real estate Web site. Click on the menu button titled "Your Own Web Site." Remember it's $24.95 to set up, and $24.95 monthly for a hosting fee.

2. Go to http://www.Barnett.PropertyFast.net to see what a functioning real estate Web site looks like. It may not be the grandest site on the Web, but it certainly gets the job done.

3. Go to http://www.AreYouDUMBEnoughToBeRICH.com to review the MY AUCTION COMPANY or MYAUC Web ware. Click on the menu button titled "MYAUC."

4. Go to http://www.AreYouDUMBEnoughToBeRICH.com and click on the menu button titled "My 1st House Auction" to see what a functioning eBay real estate auction looks like.

Remember, it is more difficult to find buyers than it is to find sellers. Don't let the names and contact information of buyers you come into contact with slip through your fingers. Even if the property they call about isn't the right one for them, you may have something else they are looking for.

Days Sixty to Ninety: Expanding into Other Real Estate Investments

As you develop your business, consider other kinds of real estate investments that can supplement your income. Here are a few ways to get started.

FINDING PRIVATE MORTGAGES

Go to the courthouse and go through the records of mortgages. Collect a number of names of private mortgage holders and the properties they own.

Look these people up and then call using this script:

> "Hi, my name's _____. I was at the courthouse today looking through public records and noticed that you provided a private mortgage on the property located at [give the street address of the property here]. My partner and I buy private mortgages for all cash. And I was just wondering if you'd like to sell yours for all cash?"

This simple action can make you $500 to $4,000 in the next thirty days. It is a powerful way to earn more cash in real estate.

LIENS

As I mentioned before, I never put my own money into real estate deals.

Let me remind you of the process here. I can provide a service to investors who are looking for a better return than they have been getting in the stock market. As we mentioned in Chapter 17, more than a *trillion dollars* left the stock market between 2000 and 2003. Much of that money is looking for a new home and much of that money is just gone. If I can provide investors with investments that will earn them approximately 12 to 15 percent and that has less risk, then I can have all the money I want to do real estate deals with. I will not be limited by my personal net worth or credit. When I can then invest my personal funds in state-administered investments yielding 20 percent or more, isn't that what I (and you) should be doing? You bet!

The Last 30 Days: Make Sure Your Money Is Working for You

TAXES

Action Step 1: *Fire your CPA.* Please don't lose the seriousness of this statement in my twisted sense of humor. Interview several CPAs until you find one who is a real estate investor him- or herself. It can make a world of difference for you.

Action Step 2: *Take the time.* Go to my Web site and take advantage of the *free* tax review.

Action Step 3: *Decide to listen in.* While you are on the Web site check out the *free* live weekly conference call. Decide you are going to be a part of the call for the next month. I'll promise you it will be informative, fun, and free.

Action Step 4: *Open your self-directed IRA account* at Mid Ohio Securities so you can purchase real estate and tax liens inside it.

Also make sure you take advantage of your tax credits, deductions, and depreciation.

When you assemble a dream team of professionals to work with, make sure you maximize your relationship with them. Encourage them to send deals your way and to work faster, more economically, and better.

A Few Final Words

In closing, I want to wish you lots of DUMB luck in your first 120 days as a new real estate investor. I am deeply touched that we have spent this time together. I hope I have been able to directly or indirectly create a path for you that leads to the fulfillment of your every dream. Clearly I couldn't add everything you need to know in this one book. Make sure you check out the recommended reading and resources lists at the end of this book. Also consider taking courses and being part of my national real estate conference calls. Remember, they're free.

From Me to YOU!

NOW! What are you going to do now? That is the question, and the answer to the question may very well determine your financial future. As we close out the time we've spent together through these pages, there are three things I'd like to give you.

The first is what I refer to as "The Five Wise Ways of the Wealthy." These Five Wise Ways of the Wealthy are what I have observed over the years are the keys to success of people who have been very successful in amassing money and who have very enviable lifestyles.

To begin with, the wealthy work. I know for many of you it's a shocking statement, but it's true. The wealthy work, they just work a lot smarter than we do or at least smarter than we have in the past. The wealthy work by using the "Cookie-Cutter System of Creating Deposits." The Cookie-Cutter System of Creating Deposits is much like the assembly line Henry Ford perfected so many years ago. It is a step-by-step system in which each action has been proven time and time again. Robyn Thompson (see the Resources Appendix B) does fifty-plus houses per year in a small market. Thompson has a cookie-cutter system. There are no bugs in her system. She stamps out cookies—I mean deposits—every day. She has a narrow focus with her company. She has a narrow focus because *it works*. Robyn has an assembly line of houses. She starts her assembly line with an old, run-down property on one end and cranks out $25,000 deposits on the other end. You don't have to do the same type of real estate Robyn does, but isn't a similar type of assembly line in whichever area of the business you decide to concentrate on necessary for success? Yes. Everyone I know who is wealthy uses this cookie-cutter system in their business.

Secondly, the wealthy understand what it means to *want*. The wealthy understand cash flow and know that money can run in cycles. So that their families don't *want* for anything when the cash flow cycle is in a downturn, the wealthy build a cash reserve. I've spoken about this in several places in the book: Build up enough cash to cover your lifestyle should your personal cash flow cycle slow down. If you have prepared for this possibility, you and your family will not want for anything in a down cycle. In fact, it is likely your family will not even know there *is* a cash flow down cycle simply because of your good planning. A wonderful by-product of this planning is your stress level. Your stress level will be much lower because you won't be consumed about where the money is going to come from to keep your household running.

Third, the wealthy are ready for *war*. The wealthy aren't warmongers, but they are ready for war, ready for battle. They are ready for battle should anyone, such as a hungry lawyer, attack their wealth. Believe me, there are people out there who will sue you for no reason. They just smell money. The wealthy are ready for battle should an attorney who's considering suing them come snooping around trying to find the money. As you may have guessed, I don't own anything. Period. Most of the wealthy are ready for war not because they have little or nothing to lose but because they just don't own anything. They have it in a trust.

Fourth, the wealthy use a lot of *water*. To make your lawn grow, it must be watered. The wealthy know that to make a fortune grow, they must water it. They must water their fortunes with investments. The wealthy base much of their fortunes on real estate, and they then water their fortunes with investments like tax liens and tax credits.

The final tip is this: The wealthy all know how to *weave*. The wealthy know how to weave the fruits of their success back into circulation. The late, great Cavett Robert (founder of the National Speakers Association) used to say, "You've got to circulate if you want to percolate." The wealthy know how to have their fortunes circulate. They understand they must give back. The wealthy I know are some of the most generous people you'll ever meet. I'll also tell you that the wealthy people I know are some of the happiest people I know.

The wealthy understand the truth of *give it back, it's yours*. Giving it back can happen in a variety of ways. The most basic way the wealthy give back is through their tithe. They tithe it back to their church or synagogue. The wealthy also give back to their communities, their favorite charities, and their professions. Please indulge me a few minutes longer while I prayerfully make a plea for Habitat for Humanity and the American Red Cross. There are a lot of great charities out there, but these two are the closest to my heart. Habitat for Humanity is because it is tied directly to real estate and because I completely believe everyone should have the opportunity to own their own home. I love the way Habitat is structured in that they are not giving homes away. The recipient must buy the home and must help to build it. Habitat simply opens doors that might otherwise stay closed. The American Red Cross desperately needs your help. Please give blood. When someone is in need of blood, there is nothing else that will take its place. They either get blood or they die. Don't worry, the Red Cross won't allow you to give too much. You can only give life through your blood every fifty-seven days. So learn to make your budding fortune grow by watering it and learn to give it back.

The next thing I want to give you is my "Special Challenge." I first shared this challenge in my book *The Great Communicators* (Royal Publishing). This isn't a challenge to make a million dollars in the next twelve months, although you can. This isn't a challenge to become an Asset or Equity Millionaire in the next 120 days, although you can. This is a challenge I hope you'll accept. This is a challenge to tell others. However, it is a challenge to tell others by sitting down over the next forty-eight hours and writing ten letters. Ten handwritten letters. They don't need to be long, but they do need to be to the point. The point of this challenge and of these letters is to let the ten most influential people in your life know how you feel about them. Take a few minutes out of your busy life and write a letter to these people. They must still be living. Tell them point-blank that you love them. Thank them for the example they have set for you and for others. Tell them about at least three specific ways in which they have influenced you. *But tell them and tell them in writing.* Please do not use e-mail or the phone for this. There is something so much more personal and meaningful about a handwritten letter. Make this a part of your life each year. You will never regret it. God bless you, and happy investing.

Chapter Summary

If you want to become wealthy, you need to act like the wealthy. Follow the Five Ways of the Wealthy and you too will be able to celebrate your three stages of being a millionaire.

The last thing I want to give you is my warmest and personal thanks. Over the last few years I've had the distinct privilege of meeting many of you and the honor of teaching you these and other exciting strategies. For those of you I haven't met in person and for whom this book has been our way of introduction—thank you. I hope you'll allow me to sign your copy soon and personally shake your hand. Mine is a wonderful life and you've had something to do with that. Please take what you've learned, put action with it, and write your own story. I remain yours in prosperity and friendship, Bill Barnett.

APPENDIX A: Pitfalls Recap
And a Few More Handy Tips

PARTNERS ARE NOT NECESSARY FOR SUCCESS IN THIS BUSINESS. They are very expensive if they are only bringing money to the partnership. I will show you how and where to find investment capital in Chapter 2. The easiest and most expensive trap to fall into is the offer of "You find the deal, you do all the work, I'll put up the money, and we'll split the profits." Although this is very fair for other types of businesses, it is way too costly for real estate. You can find other, cheaper money, as we will discuss later.

DON'T FORGET "THE MILLIONAIRE'S LEGACY." It does not take a bunch of cash, a large credit line, or a fancy office to make this business very profitable. The legacy is that you can make money, and lots of it, starting with zero. Millionaires can create money from thin air. That is what we do when we create a cash profit from an investment in which we have none of our own money. The key phrase is *none of our own money.*

DON'T BE TOO LAZY TO WRITE OUT YOUR GOALS. Written goals are a must if you are going to reach your maximum level of success.

Take the time to create a sheet of Top 10 Goals for your life and your business. Make each goal as clear as possible. Be concise and be specific.

DON'T FORGET TO USE YOUR PLAN. Plan for your success by knowing exactly how many houses you must buy and how much profit you need per transaction to fulfill your plan. Keep your plan handy—you will refine the techniques used for its attainment daily.

DON'T LET SOMEONE STEAL YOUR TENT by overlooking the obvious.

YOU DON'T HAVE TO BE THE BIG DOG TO GET RICH IN THIS BUSINESS. Please remember, it only takes a few deals a year to completely change your financial future.

DO NOT GET LAZY WHEN IT COMES TO TAX APPRAISALS. Only base your buying decisions on the value established for the property through comparable sales (comps).

DON'T FORGET THE WOW SYSTEM. This easy system will allow you to get the information you need to size up a deal quickly and easily.

MAKE SURE PROPERTY TAXES ARE PAID. On a property where the taxes are *not* escrowed, always make sure the taxes are *paid* and not simply current. Please remember there is a difference, and that difference could save you or cost you $10,000 or more.

PARTNERS—THE BIG LIE! Remember, don't get suckered in with the offer of, "I'll put up the money, you do the work and we'll split 50/50." There are plenty of hard-money investors and private investors you can deal with for a lot less money.

DON'T FORGET TO USE THE SCRIPT. Memorize this until you can say it in your sleep and in a completely conversational tone. "I know this is not for you, but who do you know that might be interested in earning 12 to 15 percent on their money, secured by a first lien on real estate for a short-term investment, six to twelve months?"

IT'S NOT THAT EASY! Yes it is! Don't allow yourself to overcomplicate this business.

PREJUDGING. Never try to determine what is best for the seller or an investor. Play the numbers game by using the script with everyone you know.

DON'T BUY OWNER-OCCUPANT HUD HOUSES. Never, under any circumstances should you try to buy an owner-occupant HUD home if you aren't going to live in it. Uncle Sam refers to this as fraud, and he tends to get pretty nasty about it.

DON'T FORGET THE LIFETIME TRANSFERABLE WARRANTY. When we are having the foundation on a property repaired, the most important factor may be the Lifetime Transferable Warranty. *Never* have foundation repairs done unless the repairing company can provide you with a Lifetime Transferable Warranty.

DON'T RELY ON THE TAX-APPRAISED VALUE OF THE PROPERTY. Please don't be lazy! Remember the only true way to establish the market value of a property is through the use of comparable sales or comps.

THE GENERAL CONTRACTOR/HANDYMAN TRAP. Remember: The person we are looking for is the handyman. If the contractor is driving the new, extended-cab, long-bed, dual-rear-wheeled Silverado pickup, that's not our guy. We want the handyman with the truck voted most likely to be mistaken for Sanford and Son's. Make sure it's you and not the contractor making the huge profits on this deal.

STAY OUT OF THE WAY. Our job is to become a professional checkwriter, not to be able to build a house from the ground up using only a Swiss

Army knife. Let the contractors do their job and you do yours. Yours is to make more offers. Period.

DON'T HIRE LANDSCAPERS. When building your rehabilitation team, in most cases there is no need for a landscaper. Remember: The yard needs to look clean and neat and have a dash of color. It doesn't take a high-priced landscaper to accomplish this.

DON'T MAKE IT TOO NICE. For some reason—maybe it's common sense—the women in my training sessions all over the country have a good handle on NOT overspending on the rehabilitation. Remember: You are not going to live there.

TURN OFF THE POWER. There are enough surprises in rehabbing a house; there's no need to make it a shocking experience also.

DON'T MAKE IT TOO BRIGHT AND CLEAN. We are walking a delicate line here between "bright and clean" and "cold and austere."

MAKE SURE YOU FIND OUT HOW THINGS WORK IN YOUR STATE. Do your homework assignment and find out. Don't be lazy. There is too much money in our business for you not to get involved.

OUR MARKET IS RED HOT SO THERE CAN'T BE ANY FORECLOSURES. Do not be lulled into the false notion that just because you live in an area where the real estate market is red hot, there are no foreclosures. Quite the opposite is true.

THE INABILITY TO CLOSE. Don't ever submit a contract on one of these deals if you aren't sure you will be able to close.

YOU'D BE LOCO NOT TO GO LOCAL. I believe you will be better served by using a local service

STAY AWAY FROM SKINNY DEALS. One of the leading reasons people fail in our business is that they jump all over a deal because it's available and not because it's a good deal.

NOT GETTING ENOUGH INVESTOR CASH TO COVER IT ALL. Remember that when we are agreeing on the amount of money our private investor is going to put up, we must make sure we take everything into consideration.

THE LURE OF THE BIG-DOLLAR HOUSE. High-end homes will put you out of business in a hurry.

CASH FOR KEYS. Don't ever hand over the money until you have the keys and the tenant is out.

THE NOSY NOTARY. The notary public is not verifying the validity of the document or contract or anything said in the contract. He or she is only verifying that the signatures on the document or contract were made by the parties to the contract.

A VALID LIEN. For any lien to be valid and enforceable it MUST be filed at the courthouse.

TIMELY PAYMENTS. If you are buying a property subject to and start having to make payments on the underlying mortgage, whatever you do, do not allow any of those payments to be late. They MUST be on time.

I KNOW HOW THEY FEEL. Everyone does not value real estate the same way we do. Your business is going to run a lot more smoothly, and you will keep from pulling your hair out if you just understand and accept this basic truth. We do not know how other people feel or what is going on in their lives, and therefore we can never prejudge another person.

THE SAME MORTGAGE COMPANY RED FLAG. If they go back to the same mortgage company, it could create questions about the sale that most sellers aren't capable of answering. The mortgage company may decide to call the loan even though you are paying the mortgage on time. The seller could also get frustrated if they can't quickly and easily explain what they are doing with you, and the entire deal could fall apart here.

THE SELLER'S BIG FEAR! Remember, by providing the seller with a purchase and sale agreement, the underlying mortgage in their name becomes offset by our payment and does *not* affect their ability to purchase another home.

THE TWO-MORTGAGE DILEMMA. The special dilemma that exists if the seller returns to the same mortgage company for their new loan that provided their old loan.

THE EMBARRASSMENT FACTOR. Don't overpay for a property just so you won't be embarrassed by making a lowball offer. Never try to judge what is in the seller's best interest or which offer they will prefer.

DEAL-ITUS. Do not work for less than 20 percent of the total value of the property just because you currently don't have a deal. Yes, there are exceptions, but please remember this guideline.

NO SURPRISE FACTOR. No matter how good you are in this business, you will never be able to cover every contingency on every deal. Accept it and be prepared.

TOO LAZY TO PACK UP AT THE END OF THE DAY? IT'LL COST YOU! Don't allow yourself or your contractors to get lazy and leave tools lying around the job site. It will invite petty thieves to break into your property, and it will slow down the entire rehab process.

KNOW THE RULES ABOUT SIGNS. Be sure to find out about any restrictions the neighborhood may have regarding the use of multiple signs in the yard.

THE NEED TO SHOW THE HOUSE. The cheapest employee you will ever have is the lockbox you purchase from a home improvement store.

Do not let buyers waste your time with property showings. Remember: if they don't know it's the kitchen without us having to show them we're not going to sell them the house anyway.

I ALREADY HAVE A CONTRACT, THANKS FOR CALLING. Make sure you build a buyers' list. Remember: It is easier to find houses than it is to find buyers for houses. Don't throw any away.

DON'T BE CHEAP. Understand that it is going to cost you to build your million-dollar-plus business. It is called, "the cost of doing business." Spend a little and earn a lot. You do not have to use the folks I recommend, but you do have to use somebody.

eBAY AND REAL ESTATE. Learn how to hold auctions on eBay for the down payments on your properties. Also, if you have friends who are real estate brokers and agents, buy them a copy of this book, you may be helping to keep their kids fed.

IT'S PASSED DIRECTLY TO YOU. It doesn't matter whether the lien price includes lawyer fees, penalties, etc., since these will be passed directly to the taxpayer.

BUYING LIENS FOR THE WRONG REASON. What you should be focusing on is the terrific rates of return made on tax liens. If you get the property, think of it as winning the lottery.

LOOK AND LEARN BEFORE YOU LEAP. Not every lien is a windfall. Spend the time learning the bidding system in the state *before* buying. It is possible, though not likely, that the property might not be worth the amount of the lien.

DO YOU HAVE THE DOUGH? Don't make a bid if you can't pay for it. It would really be embarrassing to get sued by the county.

THE BIG 8, I MEAN THE BIG 6, OH, WHO CARES? Stay away! In the last couple of years the integrity of the large accounting firms has been pretty damaged, so find a grizzled veteran who's been around the block a time or two. Best of all are grizzled veterans who actually own investment real estate themselves.

BUT I DO MY OWN TAXES, I EVEN HAVE SOFTWARE. Take the proverbial financial revolver away from your temple and don't walk, *run* to a competent CPA.

MAKE YOUR IRA SELF-DIRECTED. To be able to hold real estate inside your IRA account, your account must be self-directed.

BUT MY BROKER SAID IT COULDN'T BE DONE. And he or she is correct. You can't put real estate inside your IRA account with *them*. Find a broker who can do it for you.

WATCH WHO YOU TAKE ADVICE FROM. Don't allow yourself to listen to people who tell you things can't be done just because *they* can't do them. Listen to people who are doing what you want to do and doing it very successfully.

I'M SO CONFUSED, IT'S THE OPPOSITE OF LONG-TERM CAPITAL GAINS. Yes, inside our self-directed IRA account we *must* sell the property *within one year* or our IRA account will be considered a business and we will lose all of the tax benefits.

ONE GIANT PITFALL. THE MORE YOU DEPRECIATE, THE HIGHER YOUR TAX-ABLE INCOME WHEN YOU SELL THE PROPERTY. Unless you reinvest in another property or another tax shelter, you may ultimately increase your taxes. Make sure you go over this with your CPA and decide what's right for you.

THE CART BEFORE THE HORSE. Take care of first things first. Cover your daily cash needs first. Once these daily needs are out of the way and you have a solid cash reserve, *then* you can start to build your long-term wealth.

LET'S NOT GO CRAZY. All I am asking you to do is to put toys in their proper place—second. After you sell a property, please put 20 per-cent—yes, 20 percent—of the profits back into the company account. By doing this, you'll always have enough money to do little things for your business. Little things like marketing!

DON'T LET ANYONE RAIN ON YOUR PARADE! Please tell everyone you can about your desire to buy real estate, but if they are not selling you any real estate themselves, *how* you buy real estate is none of their business.

YOUR CONTINUING EDUCATION. Do not allow yourself to think you know it all when it comes to real estate. Buy more books to broaden your education. See Appendix C.

...And a Few More Handy Tips

Your first thirty days as a real estate investor may be the single most important time in your financial life.

Remember: This is a numbers game! Each year it only takes fifteen of those people out there to say "yes" to make you rich! This will help you sustain your energy when times are tough.

Property/House/Home. Whenever you are talking to a seller about his or her home refer to it as a "house" or "property" to help create emotional distance from the property. However, when you are sell-ing a property, always refer to it as a "home" to help establish an emo-tional bond with the property.

The difference between "current" and "paid." Remember when checking on a property that the property taxes can be current with-out being paid. You want them paid.

Would you take what you owe for the property? This simple question, which can be asked and answered in well under thirty seconds, will make you thousands and thousands of dollars if you just get into the habit of asking it.

New subdivision tours. Be sure to get out on a regular basis and look at new subdivisions. You'll get lots of decorating tips—and a lot of the competition for your buyer will come from these subdivisions.

When bidding on REO properties... Remember, one great way to distinguish yourself from everyone else who is bidding on these REO properties is to offer a fifteen-day closing date.

A great opportunity. If you are looking for a personal residence, I believe that now until the end of 2005, will offer unprecedented opportunities to purchase a foreclosure or pre-foreclosure.

Foreclosure Is a (Financial) Fate Worse Than (Financial) Death (Bankruptcy). Avoid it at all costs and help other people avoid it by offering them pre-foreclosure deals.

APPENDIX B: Resources

INVESTMENT CLUBS

Tenant Check. Sue Braun (800) 922–2214. Call Sue to find the location of your nearest real estate investment club. Remember that Sue will be a great asset to you as you build your rental portfolio. She can screen your prospective tenants quickly and inexpensively.

AIREO. Dallas Association of Independent Real Estate Owners Web site is www.AIREO.com for questions about how to start your own investment club.

REHABILITATION

Robyn Thompson is "The Queen of Rehabs." Web site address is www.RobynThompson.com

Mark Victor Hansen's Web site is www.markvictorhansen.com

HUD HOUSING

http://www.hud.org

CREATING A WEB SITE

Tim Yandell, president of INET, a Florida-based Web site design and hosting company, has put together a terrific team dedicated to the real estate investor. http://www.fastcashdirect.com/home.cfm

PRE-FORECLOSURE LISTS

If you would like to see the type of information a quality service will provide go to www.flsonline.com and check the services they provide. You will be able to see the type of information your local service should be providing.

INVESTING REAL ESTATE INSIDE YOUR IRA

Dick Desich is the president of Mid Ohio Securities, a retirement account custodial firm specializing in the intricacies of holding real estate inside your IRA. At the time of this writing, Mid Ohio has been in business for more than 27 years. Mid Ohio Securities, P.O. Box 1529, Elyria, Ohio 44036. Phone: (440) 323-5491 Fax: (440) 323-4529

APPENDIX C: Suggested Reading

Allen, Robert G. *Nothing Down.* Web site: www.RobertAllen.com

Allen, Robert G. *Nothing Down for the 90's.* Web site: www.Robert Allen.com

Barnett, G. William II. *One Hour Destiny: How to BE, DO & HAVE Everything You Want.* Web site: www.onehourdestiny.com

Edwards, Kenneth W. *Your Successful Real Estate Career.* 4th ed. New York: AMACOM, 2003.

Klauser, Henriette Anne. *Write It Down, Make It Happen: Knowing What You Want—and Getting It!* New York: Scribner, 2000. Web site: www.henrietteklauser.com

LeGrand, Ron. *Fast Cash with Quick-Turn Real Estate.* Web site: www.SDIWealthInstitute.com

Tracy, Brian. *Focal Point: A Proven System to Simplify Your Life, Double Your Productivity, and Achieve All Your Goals.* New York: AMACOM, 2002.

APPENDIX D: The Business Card

We Buy Houses
CASH

Are You Making Payments On A House You Can't Sell?

If your house is in good condition, we have solutions.

We will lease your house, make your payments, be responsible for all maintenance, pay cash when we buy, and handle all the paperwork at no expense to you!

Call now (817) 263-2316 to find out how we can help you with these and other exciting programs.

Dear Seller:

Do you own an unwanted house and need to sell quickly? Is your house vacant? Need repairs? Are you in foreclosure? Behind on payments? Relocating? Divorce? Bad tenants? Owe liens? 100% financed? Estate sale? Fire damaged? These are common problems that can happen to anyone!

We buy houses from people in situations just like yours in almost any area or price range. We can pay all cash with no contingencies and close in a few days, if needed. We will handle all of the paperwork and make all of the arrangements.

We are not realtors. We are real estate investors, and we're associated with a group of investors that buy 5 - 10 houses per month, and would like to buy more. You'll get a quick sale with no hassles and your worries will be behind you. Call now to find out how we can solve your problem!

-Bill & Kris

P.S. Rarely do problems just go away. Call now...together we can find a solution.

See other side for more exciting programs.

Bill & Kris Barnett
6709 East Park Dr.
Fort Worth, TX 76132
817-263-2316
817-263-2318 Fax
bbarnett@dhc.net

GLOSSARY

Accelerated depreciation: Depreciation is the reduction of the value of a property as a result of the passing of time. Usually used for tax purposes, the depreciation in the value of a property may be used as a tax deduction. If a property loses its value quickly, this depreciation rate may be accelerated so that most of the value is lost in the first few years and then the depreciation rate decreases later.

Acceptance: A positive response to an offer or a counteroffer that creates a binding agreement between the parties.

Accrued depreciation: From a tax standpoint, the amount of value that of a property has already accumulated (but that has not been claimed) as a result of the decrease in the value of that property.

Accrued interest: Interest which that has already been earned but has not yet been paid.

Acquisition cost: The cost to the buyer of obtaining title to the property. Acquisition cost includes the cost of the transaction of obtaining title, including legal fees and expenses, interest charges, and taxes.

Addendum: An addition to a contract.

Adjusted cost base: This is figured out when determining capital gains or losses. It is the acquisition cost of a property, plus the cost of any improvements to the property.

Adjusted sales price: The result of estimating the value of a property using comps. Take the actual sale price of a property comparable to the subject property in the same area, then add the value of any unique extras the subject property has, then subtract the value of anything the property did does not share with the comparable property.

After-tax cash flow: The net proceeds from an income-producing property, after all costs (taxes, mortgage interest, maintenance costs, etc.) have been deducted.

Agreement of sale: A legal contract in which one party agrees to buy and another agrees to sell a property.

American Society of Appraisers: A professional society for persons involved in the appraisal of both real and personal property.

American Society of Home Inspectors, Inc. (ASHI): A professional organization for persons specializing in the inspection of the physical condition of homes.

American Society of Real Estate Counselors (ASREC): A professional society for persons specializing in helping people buy and sell homes.

Annual percentage rate (A.P.R.): A rate designed to allow for the comparison of one type of loan to another. It represents the annual cost of borrowing under a given form of loan (including in the calculation compounded interest, cost of borrowing, etc.).

Appraisal: An estimation of the value of a property given by a qual-

ified person after an inspection of the property.

Appraised value: The estimated market value of a property on a given date, given by a qualified person after an inspection and a consideration of other market forces.

Appreciation: The increase over time in the value of a property caused by such things as market conditions, inflation, and changes to area around the property.

Asking price: The price at which the seller advertises a property.

Assessed value: The value assigned to a given property by the county or state for the purpose of establishing real estate taxes.

Auction: The process of selling property to the highest bidder.

Bankruptcy: The state of being unable to pay your debts wherein you submit yourself to the protection of the state. Once you are in bankruptcy, none of your former creditors may pursue you for your former debts.

Beneficiary: A person or corporate entity entitled to receive money or assets from a trust or an estate under a will.

Bid: An offer of a certain amount for a property.

Bill of sale: Documentary evidence that title to personal property (chattels) has passed to the buyer for valuable consideration.

Blood, Sweat, and Tears (BST) Value: The Blood, Sweat, and Tears (BST) Value is the value of the property after the repairs and rehabilitation.

Borrower (mortgagor): The person or company that receives money from a lender in exchange for a written promise to pay and a registered lien on property.

Broker: A mortgage broker brings borrowers together with lenders; a real estate broker brings buyers together with sellers. A broker usually charges a percentage of the contract price as a fee. Specific training is required to become a real estate broker.

Buy-back agreement: A contract between a buyer and seller in which the seller agrees to repurchase the property from the buyer if a certain event occurs within a specified period of time. The buy-back price is usually set out in the agreement.

Buyer's market: A condition of the real estate market where there are more properties for sale than people interested in buying them.

By-laws: Rules enacted by a governing body of general application.

Call option: A lender's right to demand payment of the outstanding balance of the loan.

Cancellation clause: Provision in a contract that gives one or more parties the right to terminate the contract if a specific event occurs.

Capital asset: A property to which certain tax rules (i.e., capital gains and capital losses) apply.

Capital expenditure: Money spent to improve a property and enhance its value over an extended period of time. May be added to the adjusted cost base of the property improved or depreciated over the useful life of the improvement.

Capital gain: An increase in value of a capital property (one other than a principal residence) upon which tax is payable.

Capital improvement: Value-enhancing work carried out on a property.

Capital loss: Decrease in value of a capital property. May be set off against capital gains or against regular income according to the tax rules.

Cash flow: Description of the net income from a property after all expenses of holding and carrying the property are paid.

Cash reserve: An amount of money that the buyer of a property still has after the transaction closes.

Certificate of title: A written opinion of the quality of a person's ownership of property, issued by a lawyer or a title insurance company after a search of the title records has been conducted.

Certified home inspector: A person who has met the requirements to be certified to inspect the physical condition of homes.

Certified residential appraiser: A person who has met the requirements to be licensed to appraise the value of residential properties.

Certified residential broker (CRB): A person who has met the requirements of the Realtors National Marketing Institute.

Clear title: Ownership of land that is marketable and free of competing claims, liens, mortgages, or other encumbrances

Closing: The culmination of any transaction in which the interested parties exchange documents, funds, and property and, if necessary, register the transfer of title.

Closing costs: Moneys expended by a party in completing a transaction including: legal fees, taxes, mortgage application charges, interest adjustments, registration fees, appraisal fees.

Closing date: The date set in the Agreement of Purchase and Sale upon which the transaction is to be completed, the purchase price paid, and the transfer of title registered.

Contract: A legally binding contract that must include consideration, an intention on the part of all parties to be bound to the contract, and an element of clarity such that the terms of the contract may be interpreted, understood, and enforced by a court.

Contractor: A tradesman who works in the construction industry under a contract with the owner of the property.

Credit history: A statement of the debts and obligations of a person that helps a lender to assess the risk of a loan to that person.

Decree of foreclosure: An order of the court setting out the amount outstanding on a delinquent mortgage and ordering the sale of the property to pay the lender.

Deed: The instrument by which title to property is conveyed from one person to another.

Deed in lieu of foreclosure: A legal instrument in which a borrower conveys property to a lender under a mortgage to save the expense of foreclosure.

Default: In mortgages it means the failure to make payments in full, on time, or at all or to live up to any other obligations placed on the borrower by the loan agreement.

Deferred maintenance: A nice way to say that the property has not been kept up and is depreciating.

Delinquency: The condition of being late on a payment but not yet in default.

Department of Housing and Urban Development (HUD): A federal agency focusing on programs regarding housing and renewal of city communities.

Deposit of title deeds: When a lender requires that ownership documents to be left with it as further security for a loan.

Depreciable basis: The initial acquisition cost of an improvement on land, used for income tax purposes.

Depreciation: The lessening of the value of a property over time. Also the tax adjustment for the reduction in value of an asset over time.

Equity: The difference, in dollars, between the market value of a property and the principal still owing on debts secured against the property. This is the amount of money the owner will be able to keep from a sale transaction once the mortgages are paid out.

Equity loan: A loan to a homeowner secured against the equity.

Escrow: The transfer of consideration, benefits, legal rights, money, documents or other valuables to another party in advance of that party's legal entitlement to them.

Escrow agent: Any independent third party who receives items to be held in escrow, holds such items until transfer is allowed, and then delivers them.

Eviction: The forced removal of a tenant from occupation of a property.

Fair market value: The value of an item determined by how much an independent buyer would pay for it to an independent seller in a completely free transaction.

Federal tax lien: An encumbrance registered on title to a property securing a tax debt owed by the property owner to the national government.

Finance charge: The total cost, in dollars, of a loan or mortgage over its life.

First lien: The registered legal claim that stands first in line to enjoy the proceeds of a sale of the property.

First mortgage: A mortgage that, when registered, is first in line on the property, giving the lender superior right to the proceeds of the sale of the property over other claimants.

Foreclosure: An enforcement process in which the lender under a defaulted mortgage takes title to the property for the purposes of selling it to recoup moneys owed under the mortgage.

Good faith estimate: A written statement of the anticipated costs of completing a loan transaction.

Holdback: A percentage of a contract price which that is retained by a contractor or lender until the project is completed and all bills for that project are paid.

Improvements: Things added to land to increase its usefulness and value, such as buildings, sewage, or drainage works.

Income property: A property that is owned or developed specifically to produce income for its owner.

Investment property: Real estate that is owned for the purposes of financial gain, either through appreciation or through income from the property

Judgment: A decision made by a court. If a monetary award is involved, it may become a lien on property owned by the losing party.

Judicial foreclosure: The act of selling the property to recover the mortgage debt after obtaining judgment of a court.

Lease with option to purchase: A rental contract that allows the tenant to purchase the property during the period of the lease. Payments under the lease may be credited against the purchase price.

Letter of intent: A written indication to the owner of property that the writer will be making an offer to purchase the property.

Lien: See First Lein.

Lien holder: The person who has the claim against the property.

Lien waiver: The surrender or passing up on one's right to a claim.

Listing: A real estate professional markets a property using a service. Could also be the actual notice of the property's availability and features.

Market value: An estimation of the price that could be obtained for a property if it were sold in the current market.

Monthly housing expense: The total of the costs of maintaining a home per month, including financing, realty taxes, and house insurance.

Mortgage: A loan that is secured against property (i.e., registered on title as a claim or encumbrance on the property).

Multiple Listing Service (MLS): A service created and run by real estate professionals that gathers all of the property listings into a single source.

Notice: Written warning to another of a person's or corporation's intention to take legal action.

Payment penalty: The fee paid by a borrower when he or she pays out some or all of the principal of a loan after it is overdue.

Permit: A government body's written permission to do something.

Pre-foreclosure sale: The sale of a property by a delinquent borrower under an agreement with the lender.

Property tax: The tax levied on ownership of property.

Real estate agent: A trained professional involved in the purchase, sale, and marketing of real property.

Real estate broker: A real estate professional licensed to run a real estate firm, to hold trust funds, etc.

Realtor: Professional designation for a member of the National Association of Realtors or its affiliated local groups. Must be a real estate broker.

Subject to: An indication that title to a property includes an obligation of some sort.

Subject to mortgage: A term of an agreement which states that the buyer will assume an existing mortgage registered on title to the property.

Surveyor: A professional who is trained to accurately map out land and improvements to land.

Tax lien: A claim registered against a property by a government authority for non-payment of assessed taxes.

Title: The legal term for ownership interest in land.

Title company: A corporation that is in the business of selling insurance policies of insurance guaranteeing the ownership and quality of title to land.

Title search or examination: The act of examining in detail the public records relating to ownership of a property to ensure that the current owner has clear title. Usually performed by a lawyer, qualified title searcher, or title insurance company on behalf of a proposed buyer.

Wraparound mortgage: A secondary financing option in which new money borrowed is blended with money already owed and registered on title to the property.

INDEX

ABOUT THE AUTHOR

G. William Barnett II (Fort Worth, TX) used the system outlined in this book to become a real estate millionaire in 120 days! Since 1997, he and his wife, Kris Barnett, have been buying and selling properties in the Dallas/Fort Worth area. He is currently Director of Acquisitions at CAPSTONE Properties Group.

Some of the luminaries Barnett has worked with or shared the speaking platform with include Robert Allen, Mark Victor Hansen, Zig Ziglar, Wally "Famous" Amos, Paul Harvey, Art Linkletter, Dr. Norman Vincent Peale, Dr. Robert Schuller, Earl Nightingale, Remington Shaver's Victor Kiam, and Chili's founder Norman Brinker. Before establishing himself as a real estate investor, Barnett was a nationally syndicated television producer whose story was chronicled in the book *The Great Communicators*. For fun he has served as a scout for a major college football bowl game and even spent two years as a pit crewmember for an Indy Racing League Team. This real estate investor's past includes failures as well as successes. Barnett shows you that "It only takes a small dose of success coupled with a marginal shift in thinking to change your destiny."